# PRINCES, FROGS & UGLY SISTERS

## The Healing Power of the Grimm Brothers' Tales

Other books by **Allan G. Hunter**
*Stories We Need to Know*
*The Six Archetypes of Love*
*Write Your Memoir*
*The Sanity Manual*
*From Coastal Command to Captivity*

# PRINCES, FROGS & UGLY SISTERS

## The Healing Power of the Grimm Brothers' Tales

Dr. Allan G. Hunter

FINDHORN PRESS

The right of Allan G. Hunter to be identified as the author
of this work has been asserted by him in accordance
with the Copyright, Designs and Patents Act 1998.

Published in 2010 by Findhorn Press, Scotland

ISBN 978-1-84409-184-3

A CIP record for this title is available from the British Library.

Edited by Nicky Leach
Cover & interior design by Damian Keenan
Printed and bound in the USA

1 2 3 4 5 6 7 8 9 17 16 15 14 13 12 11 10

Published by
Findhorn Press
117-121 High Street,
Forres IV36 1AB,
Scotland, UK

*t* +44 (0)1309 690582
*f* +44 (0)131 777 2711
*e* info@findhornpress.com
www.findhornpress.com

# CONTENTS

Acknowledgments ........................................................................ 7

**Introduction**
Why We Need Fairy Tales ........................................................ 9

1 **"The Frog-King"**
It's All About Sex ...................................................................... 27

2 **"Faithful John"**
A Story of Parents, Jealousy, and Pride ................................ 35

3 **"Brother and Sister"**
Boy and Girls Grow Up Differently
and see Marriage Differently .................................................. 49

4 **"The Three Spinners" and "Rapunzel"**
The Nature of the Tales and
Thwarted Young Love .............................................................. 57

5 **"Cinderella"**
Sexual Maturation and Self-Empowerment:
The Real Story .......................................................................... 65

6 **"The Girl Without Hands" and "The Robber Bridegroom"**
The Question of Good and Evil .............................................. 75

7 **"Little Snow-White" and "Allerleirauh"**
Sexual Rivalry, Narcissism, and Incest .................................. 83

8 **"Hans the Hedgehog" and "The Donkey"**
Parental Rejection and the
Recovering of Personal Authenticity ...................................... 97

CONTENTS

9 "The Three Feathers"
The Descent Into the Self ............................................. 105

10 "The Skillful Huntsman"
Controlling the Passions ............................................. 113

11 "The Two Kings' Children"
Families and Forgetting ............................................. 123

12 Beowulf and "The Golden Bird"
The Three Tests ............................................. 133

13 "The Glass Coffin"
Growing Courage ............................................. 141

14 "Little Briar-Rose"
Family Birth Order; Sleep As Metaphor ............................................. 151

Afterword
Why These Particular Tales? ............................................. 157

Appendix
The Historical Context ............................................. 163

End Notes ............................................. 167

Select Bibliography ............................................. 173

# Acknowledgments

I owe many thanks to many people—not all of whom may have been aware at the time that their comments and guidance were so helpful to me. That is part of the joy of any project that finds itself in some sort of "flow" or synchronicity. The ideas arrive and we're not quite sure where they came from. Perhaps they come from the universe itself, or from the collective unconscious. Whatever we wish to call it, gratitude is certainly the most appropriate response.

The first person I wish to thank is Lilou Macé, who set me thinking in this direction in the first place. Laura Warrell helped to move the idea forward, and from there things gathered steam. Suzanne Strempek Shea by her generosity, insight, and enthusiasm, proved to be a friend of whom I found myself constantly saying, 'How did I get so lucky as to know someone like this?' It's a question I still ask. Professor Tom Shippey's expertise kept the enthusiasm alive, while Baptist De Pape and Han Koorneef kept me alert to the possibilities and were extemely generous with their time as we worked together.

At Curry College I was helped considerably by receiving release time to work on this project: I owe my thanks to Dr. Ronald Warners and to Dean David Potash for making this possible, and to the college's president, Ken Quigley, for his support.

The trustees of the Seth Sprague Educational and Charitable Foundation, Mrs. Arline Greenleaf, and Mrs. Rebecca Greenleaf-Clapp, were inspirations to me, as well as providing the support that allowed me to road test so many of the ideas that appear in these pages in my classes with the Honors Program at Curry College.

Thierry Bogliolo, of course, deserves a special thank you—for having faith in my projects and being the most supportive publisher any author could hope for. Gail Torr—simply the finest publicist in the business—receives warm thanks and heartfelt hugs. In addition, Nicky Leach, my editor, did stellar work on the text, while Damian Keenan worked splendidly to create a cover.

People who provided inspiration include Marlena Erdos, Kelly Ferry, Briana Sitler, Simon Mason, Andrew Peerless (of Oxford University Press), David Whitley (of

Homerton College, Cambridge University), and of course my wife, Cat Bennett—our conversations each evening about the Grimm brothers' tales were a delight and a source of insight for which I shall be forever grateful. Anna Portnoy and Nick Portnoy loaned me more support than they perhaps recognize and they deserve my particular gratitude. Sally Young of Harvard University, a genius at bringing ideas forward, deserves a special mention, and special gratitude, too.

# Why We Need Fairy Tales

*Truth, naked and cold, had been turned away from every door in the village. Her nakedness frightened the people. When Parable found her she was huddled in a corner, shivering and hungry. Taking pity on her, Parable gathered her up and took her home. There she dressed Truth in Story, warmed her, and sent her out again. Clothed in Story, Truth knocked at the villagers' doors and was readily welcomed into people's houses. They invited her to eat at their table and to warm herself by their fire.*

— *JEWISH TEACHING STORY* [1]

Some years ago I was invited to give a presentation to an organization called The Man Panel.[2] I'd been asked to speak about the obstacles men and women tend to run into when they go out looking for a significant other. Just before we began, one of the organizers—a strikingly beautiful young woman in her thirties—turned to me and said: "Just so you know: these people here tonight, they're all tired of being Cinderellas. And so am I. I want that fairy godmother, and I want that prince to turn up, and soon."

I looked at her and smiled. "It sounds like you only know the Disney version of the story," I commented. "If you go to the original version—the Grimm brothers' version—there's no fairy godmother."

The woman looked shocked, her eyes wide. "No fairy godmother?" she exclaimed.

"That's right. And there's no pumpkin that turns into a coach, either," I continued. "What's more, Cinderella doesn't sit around waiting for the prince. She takes her courage and she goes out to find him."

"She does?"

"She most definitely does, and not just once but three times. The real tale will tell you what you'll need to do to be successful in love, but you have to know what it says and forget the saccharine Disney version. That version will tell you nothing."

She looked at me and nodded slowly. "I guess I'll have to take another look at that," she said.[3]

I could give many examples of this sort of conversation, but they'd all point the same way. They've shown me, again and again, how we've been misled by the sanitized versions of the old fairy tales. We've assimilated the commercialized versions, while the real tales—full of wisdom—remain unread. It's time to redress the balance. If we guide our thinking by referring to the wrong stories, then we do ourselves no favors.

## Folktale Wisdom

For generations, some of the most perceptive thinking about what it means to be a human being has been encoded in a very compact form: folktales. Not all are of the very highest quality, to be sure, but many most assuredly are. This wisdom has been understood by generations of entranced listeners and readers, regardless of intelligence, class, status, age, or ethnicity. In fact, it seems that the less well read an audience is, the greater the likelihood that a fairy tale will have real resonance and impact. Children everywhere are proof of that. The tales have given pleasure and delight, and ultimately many of them have been a source of real knowledge for generations of people who had no psychology textbooks to reference and no certified therapists to consult.

At their best, folktales show us situations of some drama—a stepmother who wants to kill her child, for example, in "Little Snow-White". Then, instead of showing the reader how to eliminate the stepparent (which is what a modern story or a video game might do), the folktales are directed toward showing a way out of the problem, thereby bringing healing to the persecuted individual. Killing a troublesome parent might seem like a good idea at the time, but as we are all well aware, it doesn't cure anything. Some of these tales—the very best ones—are healing stories for difficult personal transitions and for psychic trauma. In this book, we'll be focusing on them.

## Healing Stories

What makes a story a healing story? First, it has to depict a situation in a recognizable way. A large component of emotional healing is in the sufferer's recognition that he or she is not alone in having this particular problem; knowing that others have been down this path and have survived can be empowering. That's what members of a support group do: they exchange stories of their experiences and gain a sense of solidarity. Stories like those the Grimm brothers give us can certainly work in this way. Second, in order to aid healing, the story has to offer a possible solution or a series of insights or techniques that give the individual a sense of what to do. The Grimm brothers' tales, at their best, do exactly that, but we have to know how to recognize those insights. This requires us to think in terms of metaphors. This book is designed to help us see these metaphors more clearly.

It is unfortunate that the core truths in these stories, which were once understood in an intuitive and holistic way, have been carelessly discarded in more recent times. In some cases, the stories have been "modernized." Witness the manner in which Walt Disney Pictures has rewritten the plot of "The Frog-King" and renamed it "The Princess and the Frog" for the release of the 2009 film. The altered title alone alerts us to the different emphasis. In fact, the "princess" in this new version isn't a princess at all, and when she kisses the frog (and the kiss isn't in the Grimm brothers' version), she herself turns into a frog! In this kind of creative reworking, the insights in the original tale are too often sent to the scrap heap unexamined, or they are dismissed as "old fashioned" or some such belittling statement.[4]

Luckily, this kind of assault has not been successful in discrediting the original fairy tales; in fact, there is increasing interest in what they have to offer. For this we can thank Bruno Bettelheim's *The Uses of Enchantment*, published in 1977, which was one of the first books that dared to take the psychological insights of popular fairy tales seriously.[5] More recently, poet Robert Bly's brilliant exposition of the Grimm brothers' tale "Iron John," in his book of the same name, has certainly helped many people to reassess the life passage of maturation.[6] Gradually we're beginning to understand the psychological insights these tales can offer us—if we're paying attention.

Some years ago it became clear to me—both in my teaching and counseling—that most people had no idea about the wealth of insights available to them in folktales, so I set myself the task of gently nudging them toward the tales. I found myself using more and more examples drawn from folktales and myths, particularly in my counseling work. I found, for example, that talking with clients about the story of "The Frog-King," or relaying to them the full version of the legend of "Echo and Narcissus," led them to see the world in entirely new ways.[7] It would have taken far longer to discuss the issues concerned without using the stories. In fact, without them, it might have been impossible to discuss the issues at all—they would have seemed too remote to most people and would have been quickly forgotten. The stories gave us a handle, something accessible for us to focus on in our discussions—and, of course, that's when the real insights began to appear. That brief legends and fables could reveal and define such powerful issues surprised me again and again.

These tales worked extremely well. Yet it was also apparent that quite a few fairy tales had been Disneyfied until they were the most dreadful form of sentimentalized rubbish imaginable. Everyone has a right to enjoy what he or she wishes, of course;

however, it seemed disgraceful to me that tales of real depth and value—life-changing tales—had been betrayed for the sake of feel-good kiddie movies. It felt as if our heritage of folk wisdom had been sold.

In this book, I'll be attempting to correct that imbalance by using as a reference point the Grimm brothers' collection of fairy tales, first published in 1812.[8]

## The Order of The Tales:
## A Necessary Digression

Any reader who goes through the Grimm brothers' fairy tale collection will find that not all the material is of excellent quality. The tales come in all shapes and sizes, and it's sometimes not easy to sort them into neat categories. Some are obviously Christian saint's tales; some are anecdotes about the nature of things, similar to Aesop's animal fables. Still others are all about "trick" endings, which have more to do with the glib resolution of the plot and a quick laugh than with anything else.

The Grimm brothers seem to have been well aware of this when they put together their famous collection. For example, they created a separate category of what they called "Children's Legends," all of which teach specific Christian morals. In their main collection they included an obvious mix of tales, though.

Immediately following the first tale, "The Frog-King," we find "Cat and Mouse in Partnership" (Tale No. 2), which is, even when viewed charitably, a simple tale about how cats and mice are never likely to get on well together. The moral is fairly clear: the world is divided into savers and spenders, and the two should not form a partnership. It's useful as a way of reflecting on any imbalanced marriage, where one partner (usually the woman) stays at home and saves, while the man goes out and uses up all their savings. But because the moral is so obvious, this second tale is eminently forgettable. It has no magic in it—unless we consider cats and mice talking meaningfully together to be magic.

The next tale the Grimm brothers chose is the curious "Our Lady's Child" (Tale No. 3), which has an overt Christian statement at the end about forgiveness, and which feels as if the doctrinal content has been grafted onto an older tale. So, in the first three tales the Grimm brothers give us three examples of folk wisdom that are so obviously completely different from each other as to signal that they knew they were dealing with material that defied easy categorization.

Then we encounter Tale No. 4, "The Story of the Youth Who Went Forth to Learn What Fear Was." This is a wonderful story that reaches into the heart of any discussion about what love is and what courage might be.

It shows us a youth who cannot feel fear. He's so fearless that when he's offered the chance to spend three nights in a haunted castle, which will win him a princess if he survives, he has no hesitation in accepting. He keeps repeating that he wishes he could know what it feels like to shudder with fear, but it simply doesn't happen. So for three nights he treats the ghosts and ghouls as if they are merely rowdy neighborhood toughs he has to put in their place. In fact, he doesn't seem to have enough imagination to be afraid. He is alarmingly literal and because of that remains unperturbed. For example, when the ghouls arrive and start playing skittles using skulls for bowling balls and dead men's legs for pins he happily joins in. He interrupts the game for a few minutes, but only to use his turning lathe to make the skulls smooth enough to roll accurately. '"There, now they'll roll better!" said he. "Hurrah! now we'll have some fun!"' Clearly this is a man with no sense of the macabre.

He survives the three nights and breaks the spell, which means he wins the princess, but it is not until he is married to her that he is made to shudder with anything resembling fear. In the tale, this is because he has a bucket of cold water and small fish emptied over him by his wife. Now this is a very odd action, and it begs for us to question it. Since this happens to him when he is in bed asleep, and it's his wife who creeps out of bed and upends the bucket over him in the middle of the night, and he calls her "my dear wife" as he shudders, it's not hard to connect this to sex. The shock of cold water would make anyone shiver, of course, but we are not in a literal world at this point; we are in a metaphorical realm. Warm in bed, the youth has his sense of security ambushed.

To understand this we have to see it as an assault on a comfortable mind-set. Which of us hasn't been awakened in the night, perhaps by a loud noise, and felt that everything we thought was rock solid might not be? Perhaps at such a moment we discover most acutely what we hold precious. Ask anyone who has awakened in the night with the fire alarms blaring. People run from their homes clutching their spouse, their children, their cat, but they tend to forget their bank statements. At such times we know whom we hold dearest, and our fear for the safety of those people is a measure of our love for them.

As we've seen in the tale, the youth has previously been holding his vigil in the castle. He's been awake and, therefore, anticipating trouble, so he's not been able to experience the shock of being propelled from sleep to waking, unexpectedly. This literal-minded, practical man has to be made to break through to the realm of the imagination, the realm of dreaming, to find out what love feels like. Once he does so, he shudders.

Symbolically, the tale makes the elegant point that love is, to a huge extent, rooted in the knowledge that life is short, love is sweet, and that it is hugely satisfying that we have been accepted by our lover. The shudder comes from the knowledge of the fragility of life and love, and that it might one day all be taken away without warning. We see this on our television sets every day. Survivors of a disaster cling to each other, suddenly made aware that they could have lost their loved ones. At such times they don't see the world in the same way.

It is a situation, we could say, that reveals the positive aspect of fear. The young man in the tale experiences the sort of fear that causes us to cherish the moment, and the shudder is of pleasure as well as of recognition. What a wonderful way to describe that feeling of lying in the arms of one's beloved, enjoying the moment, knowing that the moment will inevitably pass! Sweets tasted when one is aware of the rapid passing of time become all the sweeter. It's a magnificent psychological insight into love—and it's conveyed in a strong visual image, not in the words of explanation I've used here, which must seem clumsy by comparison.

What we can take away from this is that no one, not even the fearless man, can truly love until he's felt vulnerable. Courage, on its own, is never enough. To place vulnerability at the center of this tale is uncannily modern. There can be no love without it. Love is based in an act of imagination, which always makes us vulnerable. If it were not the case, we'd all just marry the person with the largest bank account. Yet the number of people in our world today who do not find love because they cannot let themselves be open or take the risk of being hurt is, perhaps, higher than ever. This is a tale we need today, to let us know where we so often go wrong.

Clearly this is a strong and imaginative tale. But just as we think we're moving into some interesting stories we are disappointed, for the next tale is "The Wolf and the Seven Little Kids" (Tale No. 5), which has very little to offer the reader. This is followed by "Faithful John" (Tale No. 6)—a complex tale of the psyche and parental dynamics, presented to us with plenty of magic to make the plot function. Tale No. 7 surprises us again, because it is a rather offensive tale about a peasant and the profit he unwittingly makes from a soldier and a Jew.

What are we to make of this mixture? Two possibilities spring to mind. The first is that the Grimm brothers thought all these tales were equally good and simply jammed them together. That seems unlikely. The second possibility is that the brothers knew exactly what they were doing in their arrangement.

If we scan the table of contents of their volume, we find that the tales that have captured our imaginations over the generations—"Cinderella," "Little Snow-White," and so on—are sprinkled throughout the collection in the same way that candied fruit is evenly distributed in a well-mixed fruit cake. We come across nuggets of excellence every so often, interspersed with less good material.

# Collecting Tales

In fact, the Grimm brothers worked closely with several gifted storytellers, including Frau Katherina Viehmann, who took her task very seriously and insisted on the accuracy of the versions she was telling.[9] This leads us to believe that she had a repertoire, a sequence of tales. Like any well-rehearsed performer, she aimed to please all tastes and to spread the truly excellent material throughout the evening's recitation, as a stage show might save certain star turns for specific parts of the show. This might help to explain why some of the tales are not memorable and are even of poor quality. It also helps us to see why the collection of tales tended to be disregarded in later centuries: it was hard to distinguish the wheat from the chaff.

Here, it's worth noting that the Grimm brothers were careful to record who had told them which tales, but when they produced their famous collection they mixed the tales in according to their own taste. They did not place all the tales from Katherina Viehmann together, nor did they do this for the tales supplied by the Wild family, the Hassenpflugs family, nor the Haxthausen family. They also looked through medieval manuscripts and through other collections "from the time of Luther" for likely tales.[10]

The result is that, as we read the tales, we occasionally find thematic clusters. The tales based on birds would be just one example. "The Willow Wren" (Tale No. 171), "The Bittern and the Hoopoe" (Tale No. 173), and "The Owl" (Tale No. 174) are grouped together, along with a fish tale of the same sort—"The Sole" (Tale No. 172)—just to leaven the mix.

We notice right away that "The Owl" shifts the attention from why animals either look or sound as they do to commentary about people's fearful reactions to the owl itself, so the theme of the tales slips into another realm of thought. It's a deft piece of arranging.

From this, there is really only one conclusion we can draw: the Grimms knew their tales were astonishingly varied in type, length, and worth, and they sought to give us a wide selection, knowing that a few, here and there, were magnificent. The richest of the tales always have an element of magic in them.

## The Historical Wrangles

Before we continue, I would like to acknowledge and deal with some awkward historical disputes that could sidetrack our examination of the tales. For one thing, there is the question of the provenance of the tales before the Grimm brothers collected them.

Recently the controversial Ruth Bottigheimer has attempted to show that favorite fairy tales, such as "Cinderella," were in fact invented in the sixteenth century because early printed versions of the tale exist and can be referenced.[11] This is interesting evidence but certainly not conclusive. The fact that tales were written down or published at some point does not mean that other versions were not in oral circulation, and perhaps had been for generations.

We know, for example, that much longer tales, such as *Sir Gawain and the Green Knight* (from circa A.D.1375) and *Beowulf* (probably circa A.D. 800) were in existence in oral traditions long before they were written down. In the case of *Beowulf,* enough historical references remain intact in the text that we can trace a few characters back to actual history, some two hundred years before the probable date of writing.[12]

In addition, we know that many oral stories changed as soon as they were written down. Chaucer's *Canterbury Tales* (1387), for example, gives us a very mixed bag of tales, supposedly repeated by different people on a pilgrimage. However, Chaucer is almost certainly displaying literary license and taking the opportunity to exploit a number of tales already in existence, to which he gives his own spin. To offer just one instance, he borrowed freely from Boccaccio's *The Decameron* (1349–1351), which has the same premise as *The Canterbury Tales,* except for the fact that the travelers are supposedly fleeing the plague in Florence and start to tell stories centered around love to while away the time.

There are many more examples of literary license in storytelling. Marie de France and the cycles of French *Lais* all seem to be similar in general intent, and many of these stories have sources we can trace to written versions. We know that Marie de France recited her stories at many French courts, so her tales are hardly intended for the ordinary people, the "folk." The point here is that folktales cannot be proved to be "pure" orally transmitted tales, uncontaminated by literary sources. Storytellers of all kinds have always stolen plots, themes, and entire stories. A recent case in point is Helen Fielding's *Bridget Jones's Diary*, which is a self-proclaimed adaptation of Jane Austen's *Pride and Prejudice*—a fact that helped to *increase* sales rather than diminish them.[13]

This means that, unfortunately, we cannot be completely sure about the origins of any of the tales we have grown to know and love. There simply is not enough evidence—or rather there's only enough evidence to create plenty of room for argument and disagreement.

So I'd like to suggest a way forward. Some tales are obviously so much richer than others that they stand out. Let us take the Grimm brothers as a source, imperfect but probably the best we have, and look for the deep wisdom that exists in many of the tales. The Grimm brothers were scrupulous about finding the best and most authentic versions of the tales they could locate, and we can be guided by their expertise. In the end, we do not need to know where the wisdom comes from; we need to know how we can apply it to our lives.

Think of it this way: when a ship goes down at sea, we may find ourselves swimming toward a lifeboat. When we reach the lifeboat, we don't say: "But this lifeboat doesn't seem to have come from my ship! Can I get into it? Is that allowed?" I suppose we could, if we were overly scrupulous, refuse to get into the lifeboat, and drown. That's a real choice. It's not one that I would recommend.

We could take this comparison farther and say that the ship sinking can be seen, perhaps, as the devastation wrought upon oral storytelling by important historic events during the late Middle Ages.

There were many such disruptions we can point to. To begin with there was the rise of wealth in terms of gold and silver coming from the New World after 1500. This upset the feudal economy, displaced whole villages, and eventually helped depopulate the European countryside. There was also the effect of the Reformation, which attempted to get rid of old superstitions and any stories associated with them. As if that wasn't enough there was the effect of the Counter-Reformation, which energetically crushed dissent, burned "witches" and heretics by the hundred, and quashed the telling of fairy tales thought to be ungodly. Finally, we could point to the disastrous effects of the wars and plagues that swept over Europe with some regularity.

The assaults upon literature and the telling of tales have been devastating and numerous; yet, the folktales have stubbornly survived. Things survive in a culture because they have resonance. People value folktales because they feel some sort of benefit from them.

So we could lose ourselves in the discussion of where these tales came from and in the process lose the value that exists in them for us, the readers. In one sense, it does not matter where the tales "came from." Just as Chaucer's tales may have come from a conversation he had in a pub, it is not where they originated but what has been done with them that matters. Perhaps it is better to focus on what the Grimm brothers gave us in their editions and to marvel at the virtuosity of those who told them the tales. The Grimm brothers may have been the collectors who brought us the tales, but that in no way reduces the magnitude of the tales themselves.

We know almost nothing about many writers from the past, but that in no way impedes the usefulness of their words. Shakespeare is but the most obvious example. Here was a man who stole all his plots with the possible exception of two, and about whose life and personal doings we have far more conjecture than actual verifiable fact. Did he write all the plays attributed to him? Did he collaborate with others? (The answer is yes.) Do we even have all his plays? (The answer is no.) Even his precise dates of birth and death are in doubt, to which some would add the spelling of his name and even his identity. Was he in fact the Earl of Oxford? Does it matter? Not really. The plays exist, along with the sonnets and the poems. They are what matters.

Let's agree to look at Grimms' collection of tales in the same way. We have some reliable texts of great value. Let's see what they can tell us.

## Guiding Principles

We'll be looking at some tales that will be familiar and some that will be less familiar; in each case, we'll be extracting the nuggets of wisdom within them that we may even have forgotten to seek. And we'll see that the best of these tales use the concept of the six archetypes, which may be found in the greatest literature of our civilization.

By using the term "fairy tale," I'm attempting to be specific. My focus here will be on tales in which some sort of character change or recognition takes place, usually signified by a magical event. There might not be an actual fairy in the tale, but the existence of magic is enough to allow us to call them fairy tales. The choice of the Grimm brothers' collection is apt because most people today know about fairy tales from the Grimm brothers' careful gathering of stories. I will not be attempting to trace back all the variations of the tales into the dim recesses of history. Better and more able minds have done that. Instead, I will be treating the tales the Grimm brothers chose as a more or less reliable sample of storytelling that has become, in its own right, a force within our culture. One might say that the tales in their entirety have taken on a life of their own, and it is that collective wisdom I'll be exploring.

Next, I would like to explain the term "archetypes," since I'll be using that term frequently. If you have read *Stories We Need to Know* and other books I've written, you may already be familiar with the archetypes.[14] In that case, I'd advise you to skip ahead. If not, please read on.

## The Six Archetypes

Broadly speaking, archetypes can be seen as developmental stages that every human being is called to go through and that are sufficiently strongly defined that they can be rendered in popular stories by the use of an easily recognizable figure. But please notice, an archetype is not the same as a stereotype—the "obnoxious teenager" type we see in sitcoms, for example. That figure can be seen as going through a developmental stage; however, an archetype is something more: it moves beyond easy definitions to describe the way a person is choosing to use his or her energy.

To illustrate how people use their energy, we'll need an example. Let's consider three very different people; say, a CEO, a farmer, and a tramp. Each of them is different; yet what may link them is the way they respond to the world and its challenges. Now let's imagine that each one, at his or her core, is a frightened individual. The CEO seeks to mask this fear by making money, perhaps, in order to gain self-esteem. In contrast, the farmer may fear not being seen as a good person, and so he does exactly what everyone else does in the hope that he will fit in and be accepted. Meanwhile, the tramp may also be frightened, and he may express this as a fear of settling down anywhere so he doesn't have to become accountable for his life. Three different people, three different responses, but all are an expression of an underlying attitude toward the world and a giving-in to fear.

In this particular example, despite the surface disguises, each of these people is a lost soul yearning for some place to belong. They can all be recognized as a version of the Orphan archetype—those people who prefer to try to fit in as a way of avoiding making up their own minds about who they are; they are afraid of acting in a way that is personally declarative. Like real-life orphans they need to find someone to give them security, or some lifestyle into which they can be adopted, and to achieve this they are willing to damp down their individuality.

An archetype, then, has less to do with what people are, or what they do for a living, than how they choose to face the world. It's a life attitude.

When seen in this way we discover that archetypes have widely variant forms but always correspond to the same six deep structures of personal energy. These are:

**THE INNOCENT**

**THE ORPHAN**

**THE PILGRIM**

**THE WARRIOR-LOVER**

**THE MONARCH**

**THE MAGICIAN**

These six archetypes have existed in almost all the great works in western literature for the last 3,500 years, including the New and Old testaments of the Bible, the Koran, and in many lesser works such as novels, poems, folktales, and fairy tales. They always appear in the order cited above and are always concerned with the same struggles. This seems to be pretty conclusive evidence that there is some validity to the idea.

The definition of archetype I am using here is rather different from what you will find in Carl Jung's work, and in the work of his followers.[15] I'm not attempting to disprove what Jung says; I simply wish to show that there is another aspect that he does not consider, but which has validity nevertheless. Let's look now at how the archetypes appear throughout life and in what ways they inform experience.

## Innocents and Orphans

We all start out in the world as **INNOCENTS**. As babies, we are naturally loving and trusting, and although we might not be very good at anything else, we do know how to love and trust. That may not sound very impressive, but bear in mind that it is impossible to have a successful adult relationship without the qualities of Love and Trust, which we learn to develop from birth onward.

The adult who is an Innocent will forgive easily, as a young child does who greets the returning parent with joy, no matter what sort of person the parent is. In the adult world, this can be a blessing and a curse. We need to forgive others and ourselves, but some people will then just keep on mistreating us. Innocence may be delightful, but it's a difficult life strategy. In "The Frog-King," for example, the princess is quite happy playing with her ball by the well—until it falls in. She's an Innocent on the cusp of change.

When things go wrong like this, or threaten to go wrong, we enter the **ORPHAN** stage. As its name suggests, at a certain point the disappointments of the world lead to us being ejected from the safety of the family, and we have to make our own way, find our own shelter, or ask for help. In folktales, this is often signified when a stepparent sends a child out alone into the world. "Hänsel and Gretel" is a clear example of Innocents who are led out into the world and abandoned by their parents. As Orphans they make the potentially disastrous choice of the witch's house as a place of shelter, where they are forced to do as they are told while they are being fattened up to be eaten. They find themselves "adopted" but not into the best of situations.

The Orphan can exist in other forms, too. In "Cinderella," for example, Cinderella has nowhere else to go once her mother is dead, so she is forced to stay sitting in the ashes and endure mistreatment; she is, in fact, an Orphan, even though her father is still around. But when news of the ball arrives, she realizes she has a chance to take charge of her life. This is what leads her to the next stage, the **PILGRIM**.

## Pilgrims and Warrior-Lovers

The Pilgrim sets out on a journey toward a truth with which he or she can live. This yearning for personal truth is what motivated Christian pilgrims in the Middle Ages, as they traveled to shrines as far away as Jerusalem; it's what continues to energize them today. The Pilgrim takes to the road not knowing exactly where it will lead but determined to explore whatever may happen along the way.

At the center of this experience is a working out of one's relationship to God or to the divine. Pilgrims go to Mecca each year; they travel to Benares; they visit the site of the Bo tree at which Buddha became enlightened; they walk the routes to the great cathedrals of Spain and France and other holy places to expiate sins or just as an act of devotion. In New Mexico each year the Easter Pilgrimage to the sacred Santuario de Chimayo, north of Santa Fe, often involves whole families. Some of these pilgrims carry crosses as they walk; some complete the entire journey on their knees. They arrive on Good Friday, often after having walked all night. It's a time of action and also a time of faith. But other types of pilgrimage are just as important, even if they are expressed in a more modest way.[16]

In the fairy tale of "Cinderella", for example, this pilgrimage takes the form of Cinderella going to the ball three times. She leaves the uncomfortable yet reliable shelter of her home and ventures out, so that she can meet the prince and decide if he is the person for her. She runs away from the prince three times, we notice. If she were simply desperate for a new home she'd have stuck to him right away at that first ball and not rested until she had his ring on her third finger. But what she knows is that it's not just any home she craves, but the *right* one.

This is the way of the Pilgrim. This is the person who may refuse many seemingly tempting offers because none of them feel right. Parents everywhere have been in despair at children who will not take over the family business, who refuse to accept the career that has been laid out for them, or who won't marry the nice girl/boy next door whom everyone considers a perfect match. When the Pilgrim stays faithful to the search (and not all can, or do), he or she gains confidence and can access the courage with which to face the world.

At this point the Pilgrim is ready to choose a life, and to fight for that life because it is something he or she desires and loves. This is when the individual becomes a **WARRIOR-LOVER**, a person who has a personal belief that is worth defending and who knows that this belief is worthy and compassionate. After all, you can't fight for something or someone you don't love, and you can't really love something or someone not worth the fight.

This may be the point at which a person selects a career or a life path and also chooses a life partner; in each instance, the choice will feel personally authentic. This is the person who is operating out of a core of personal strength, since the attributes of courage and of executive, decisive authority (The Warrior) will be balanced by the qualities of compassion and understanding (The Lover).

In the fairy tale of "Rapunzel," the Warrior-Lover can be seen in the person of the king's son, who even though blinded after escaping the witch in the tower, spends seven years searching for his lost love. Examples of this in our everyday world might include advocates for peace, justice, and the environment, such as Gandhi, Dr. Martin Luther King, Jane Goodall, Mother Teresa, and other figures, less famous, who have worked tirelessly to bring more harmony into the world. These are the people fighting for a worthy cause or belief who change history in a positive direction.

## Monarchs and Magicians

Sooner or later, every Warrior-Lover will have to stop being a one-person army and start to train the next generation of workers for the cause. When this happens, the next archetype comes into being: **THE MONARCH**. Like the ideal monarch, this is a person who is sensitive to the needs of the whole realm. This person will listen, assess, and then act for the best interests of all, not just a few. This is a figure tasked with distinguishing whom to trust, whom to distrust, and whom to groom for the next generation of leadership.

History is littered with examples of rulers who were unable to do this, who could not delegate duties, and who trusted no one. These sorts of rulers do not last long— nor do those rulers who just take the money and have a ball.

Just as the Warrior-Lover has to balance the stereotypical "male" and "female" attributes of decisiveness and compassion, it falls to the Monarch to recall that lesson on a larger scale in order to serve the larger good. When a Monarch is working properly in this way, the ego almost entirely disappears. The Monarch does not say, "Look what I did!" Instead, the Monarch tends to want the people concerned in a project to recognize what they all did together and see that they also are capable of doing far more.

The role of the Monarch is to organize and energize the population, not to order them around like slaves. When this happens successfully, groups of people become inspired by what they are doing and find that they are capable of far more than they had at first believed was possible. That is, one might say, a form of magic.

The leader who can cause this to happen is, therefore, at the next archetypal stage: **THE MAGICIAN**. Notice, this is not about waving a wand and making things happen contrary to the laws of nature. It's about putting people in touch with the best and strongest parts of themselves, so that change—miraculous change—happens in accordance with the laws of nature.

The Magician is the person who can change the energy of a situation, so that a better outcome can occur. We've all seen examples of this. This is the team coach who doesn't play in the game but who knows just whom to choose, what to say, and when, so that the team can become far more than its individual members had thought was possible. This is Grandma, saying exactly the right words to a child to make him stop being a nuisance, when no one else can. This is the skilled therapist who knows the precise time and the exact moment to intervene to change a life. This is Nelson Mandela moving South Africa to a peaceful power transition as all-white rule came to an end. It looks like Magic. In each case, the Magician's achievement comes from wisdom and from handing power back to the individuals concerned.

These, in a very brief form, are the six archetypes in the order they appear in life. They are present in many folktales and in the great works of literature, and we can observe them all around us every day, too. Since literature has always been a way for us to explain ourselves to ourselves, it's just possible that these six archetypes may be one of the deep structures of the human psyche—one of the ways in which we make sense of our lives. They may be an "elementary structure" of human behavior, to borrow a phrase that mythologist Joseph Campbell adapted from Adolf Bastian.[17]

## Uses of the Archetypes

One of the things my work on fairy tales has shown is that the archetypes are plentiful in many tales, but not in all. This is because some tales are actually very simple moral lessons and don't require any character development at all—thus, no archetypal growth. Characters start in one archetype and remain there at the end of the tale. However, the longer, more complex stories of psychic growth all have the archetypes within them, operating in exactly the same way.

This should not surprise us. To some extent all literature that became "great" in later generations started off as, or sprang from, folktales and fairy tales. It's not the source that matters as much as what happens to the material in the later treatment. Shakespeare and Marlowe stole their plots, for example; indeed, for many centuries, it was expected that writers would take their plots from elsewhere.

Shakespeare himself makes fun of this in *A Midsummer Night's Dream*. In it, we will recall, the amateur acting troop of Bottom and Company put on an hilarious production of *Pyramus and Thisbe*, which was an ancient tale even then. In it Pyramus and Thisbe are lovers who are forbidden to meet, so they arrange to run away and meet at night outside the city, by Ninus' tomb. Thisbe arrives first, is frightened by a lion that has just killed an animal, and runs away. The lion tears her cloak to pieces, leaving bloody tooth marks on it. Pyramus arrives later, finds the bloodstained cloak, fears the worst, and kills himself with his sword. Thisbe creeps back, finds Pyramus dead, and she, too, kills herself using his sword.

All this takes place as an incompetently acted play within the main play, and the audience on stage and the audience in the theater laugh heartily. Yet—in case we didn't notice—the events are extremely close to those experienced by the lovers on the stage who are laughing at the play within the play. Those lovers had also been forbidden to marry, and that's why they ran away into the woods at night, where confusions occurred that threatened to destroy their happiness. In fact, they've only just managed to sort all this out. The ridiculous performance by Bottom and Company is a simpler version of the main drama's plot, but with a tragic ending. It is almost as if Shakespeare is nodding to his source material and saying, this was the kernel out of which my play grew.

Stories get borrowed and expanded in this way—sometimes more than once. Shakespeare also uses a very similar plot in *Romeo and Juliet*, for example, and it is hard to say where the ancient tale starts and "literature" begins. Romeo and Juliet also flee their city and meet at a tomb at night, where Romeo thinks Juliet is dead (when, in fact, she's sleeping, thanks to a potion she's been given) and so kills himself. She then wakes up, sees Romeo lying dead, and follows suit by killing herself with his sword. It's very similar in its overall outline.[18]

A detailed search of sources might tell us more about where Shakespeare got his ideas, but it can't tell us how or why he decided on these particular stories rather than others. So let's not try to investigate literary history or read Shakespeare's mind. Let's say, instead, that in some folktales there is a germ of something that is so psychologically true and apt that it deserves notice. We could call it insight, or wisdom, or whatever we wish, but it seems to be there, which is probably why the tales have endured, and why others have found them a rich source of inspiration.

Joseph Campbell referred to the way these tales worked by saying they appealed to "the picture language of the soul," which he suggested was the same unconscious language we experience in dreams.[19] Tales such as these speak to us in a language that exists at a primal level of our awareness. This is hard to prove, but it feels true.

Perhaps it was this awareness that caused the great poet W. H. Auden to write of Grimms' collection that it is:

> Among the few indispensable, common-property books
> upon which Western culture can be founded.... It is hardly
> too much to say that these tales rank next to the Bible in
> importance.... Beautiful.[20]

Auden wrote those words in 1944, when a new edition of Grimms' Fairy tales was published. He could have sneered at them. After all, they were German in origin, and England and the United States were engaged in a ferocious war against Germany at the time. Auden himself had left England for the United States at the height of the

London Blitz, when the invasion of the British Isles seemed imminent, so he had no cause to be gentle in his views on anything German. Yet he came forward with this powerful endorsement, and he did so because he saw the genius in these stories. Thirty years later, Richard Adams of the *New York Times Book Review* returned to Auden's comments.

> Everything Auden said then remains relevant and valid.... Everyone should possess and know Grimms' Fairy tales—one of the great books of the world—and no English-speaking person could do better than this edition.[21]

This is the edition, therefore, I have chosen to use and to examine—to see what we can learn by following these claims. Like Auden and Richard Adams, I feel the tales have to be read, savored, and thoroughly known.

What we'll find will surprise us. There really is deep wisdom in many of these tales, if we care to listen for it. And it is wisdom that reaches as far into human behavior as anyone has dared to go. These are tales that deal with love, disappointment, growth, murder, guilt, forgiveness, incest, and sexual abuse. And within each tale, there is sufficient information to allow the reader to see how to heal from these unfortunate situations. Everything that we commonly think of as psychology is there. The tales also ask us to look at ourselves in a new way— a way that requires us to look past the sense of everyday concerns and practical solutions. They require us to open our hearts to metaphor.

## CHAPTER 1

# "The Frog-King"

## It's All About Sex

The very first tale in the Grimm brothers' collection is "The Frog-King." We all think we know this one. It's about the princess and the frog, and the cliché goes that you have to kiss a lot of frogs before you find a prince. Well, guess what? In the original tale, the princess doesn't kiss the frog at all, although he does change into a prince. It's only the Walt Disney version that has the frog being kissed; in creating his money-making animated cartoons, Disney betrayed the heart of the tale.

Let's take a fresh look at this tale and see whether we can learn something more useful than how to kiss amphibians.

The tale starts with a princess, the youngest of her family, who is as fair as the sun, we are told. She likes to go to the edge of "the great dark forest" and sit by the well next to a cool fountain, where she plays catch by herself with a golden ball. One day this ball falls down the well. She bursts into tears, and a talking frog retrieves it on the understanding that he will sit beside her, share her plate of food, and share her bed. Once the ball is returned to her, of course, she runs away. The frog has to pursue her and, when he makes his claim known, the king, the princess's father, says the promise must be honored.

The princess is not happy about that, of course. The frog is not very pleasant, and when he wants to share her bed, she rebels. She picks up the frog and throws it against the wall, to kill it. That's not in the Disney version—Disney has the kiss, instead. Perhaps the studio executives were afraid that rendering the Grimm version would have been tantamount to encouraging children to abuse animals. Yet this detail is the clue we need if we are to understand the tale.

The princess has to get blazingly angry before the magical change can occur. Remember, the frog is already in the bedroom with the princess when he says, "I am tired. I want to sleep as well as you, lift me up, or I will tell your father." This makes the princess "terribly angry," we are told. She doesn't just put him down on the farthest corner of the sheets; she hurls him "with all her might" against the wall.

PRINCES, FROGS & UGLY SISTERS

This sort of strong reaction is to be expected when our sexual boundaries have been breached; and yet, it's only when the princess hurls the frog at the wall that he turns into a handsome prince. Furthermore, instead of them running off to tell the king, guess what? He tells her his story about being bewitched and "then they went to sleep." It's pretty obvious that they're in the same bed. He's already said he'll take her off to his kingdom in the morning as his wife. Sex is definitely in the air, although this time it seems to be consensual.

The beauty of the tale is that it is all about sex without saying so directly. The princess is the youngest daughter and the most beautiful, and we could deduce from this that she's probably a favorite, Daddy's girl, used to getting her own way. That's why she weeps when she loses the golden ball and why she thinks she can get away with not keeping her promise to the frog.

The golden ball is, therefore, not just a stage prop. It is a symbol of her self-indulgent completeness, and the circumstances of its retrieval suggest her tendency to bend the rules to her own will. We notice, also, that she plays by herself with the ball. As we know, a sphere has only one surface to it—it is complete unto itself. The sphere is, therefore, a very good symbol of the "little world" of the self. Just as a king carries an orb, a golden symbol of the globe that suggests his role as a ruler in the larger world, so, too, the princess has her smaller golden sphere.

What all this conveys to us is that, at a certain point in childhood, we lose our sense of innocence, just as the princess loses her toy. We lose our happy self-absorption, which, until then, has had us thinking that everything would always go our way. Our sense of self has to reassess what is going on because we can't quite manage on our own any more, and that's an unwelcome surprise. In such situations, when we weep or call for help, to some extent we're annoyed that we need help at all, and so we feel some shame and disappointment about that.

This is especially true of children, who often want to be able to do things themselves. They wail when they can't manage whatever it is, then they resentfully accept help. It's the same sentiment that, later in life, stops people going to a doctor or a therapist because they feel they ought to be able to get well on their own and are annoyed that they can't. So when help comes, even though it's welcome, it tends to be seen as less than what it is, as unacceptable—an amphibian.

It is a behavior that we can see in many different guises today. I know perfectly wonderful human beings who happen to be car mechanics. Surprisingly often they've spoken about being treated like dirt by wealthy customers who can't believe their fancy car has broken down. So they take out their sense of entitled rage on the mechanic—the man who is putting things right for them. It's the same behavior as our princess displays, written larger. She wants the problem solved, she wants it solved now, and she doesn't want to acknowledge that she's a part of a wider world.

Notice, also, the detail that the well is next to the dark wood. For generations, the dark wood was seen as a place where one could lose oneself. It's a reference that will echo through almost all the tales—think of Hänsel and Gretel being abandoned, or Snow-white getting lost in the forest before she finds the dwarfs' house. Arthurian legends are replete with the same sense of the forest as being a place in which people lose their way, as well as their sense of self. So we have been primed to think of the well as being right next to a place where one could lose oneself.

When the ball falls into the well, which is "so deep the bottom could not be seen," we are already being asked to think mythically about reaching into the depth of the unconscious, that watery world of uncertainty and emotion, in order to dredge up something that has been temporarily lost. When the golden ball is returned the princess runs away, but we know that the golden ball of her restored self has in the meantime been to a dark place she is not willing to acknowledge just yet. The princess has just gone through something that will cause her to have to think about the deeper levels of her psyche, although she doesn't want to. She's discovered she needs other people, and she needs something from them she's not quite sure she can bring up in polite conversation.

When we meet people who have gone deep into the psyche—which is what the frog has done—they can seem a little bit scary. As we discover at the end of the tale, the frog was once a prince and, in his degradation, he has had to think very thoroughly about who he once was. He's faced despair and the loss of his outer identity; as a result, he's come to a place of knowledge about who he is.

This is something that the princess is not sure she wants to encounter just yet— she wants to keep on playing. So the frog sets her a test. He invites her to discover herself. We could say she's like the rich kid who gets accidentally marooned in the ghetto after dark and is rescued by a street-wise tough: her world will never be quite the same again. She may have to rethink many of her comfortable prejudices. It's quite a challenge. In conventional terms, though, she has reneged on a promise, so she has to learn that her word must be her bond.

That's not easy for her to face. She's been the indulged child, so she thinks she can get away with breaking her word. She seems genuinely surprised when her father, the king, insists that she should do the honorable thing. He has to "command" her to let the frog into the castle, as the story tells us.

Remember, this is Daddy's girl, and she expects to get away with things. She has a rude shock. Sulkily, she agrees to do as her father says. She even tries tears, but the king, we are told, "grew angry and said: 'He who helped you when you were in trouble ought not afterwards to be despised by you.'" It's a straightforward moral lesson of respect and gratitude.

The frog, at this point, *seems* to behave like the quintessential creep. He's like a man who manages to ingratiate himself with a young woman, making her feel obliged to him in various ways, and who waits around, using a kind of social blackmail, until the woman eventually agrees to have sex with him. This is not pushing things too far. I'm sure we've all seen this. It's pretty common. If we need proof, then we have only to think of the number of women who, today, will not let a man pay for their dinner because they do not wish to be under any sort of obligation to him, let alone one that could be sexually coercive.

Well, the frog is definitely behaving like one of those sexually coercive kinds of men. And here's the point: it's not until the princess gets angry that things can then change. She could just have gone along weakly with what her father demanded, and with what the frog could coerce her into, in which case she'd have been a person of no spirit at all, and not worth knowing, let alone marrying.

Instead, she finds her inner strength. She breaks away from her father's words. She rebels against the frog's insistence and throws him at the wall. That's when she says, in effect, that she knows someone has to be in her bed, but that that doesn't deserve it to be a frog! She deserves better! It's only when we demand better that we show our real quality.

The princess is not just being a prima donna; she's actually got some standards. That's why she's now worth loving—and why the prince can emerge. That's the nature of the test he sets her. In everyday terms, we might say that people behave about as well toward us as we are prepared to put up with. A spouse or significant other who is not behaving properly won't shape up unless some real anger is expressed.

The princess has learned a vitally important life lesson. Anger can be productive, even necessary, and it can cause real change to occur when we decide not to accept less than we deserve. It's a valuable lesson even today. The number of people who accept far less than they deserve in their significant others is still a sad fact of modern life. These are the people who settle for what's on offer, who marry because they can't seem to find anyone else, who are abused and betrayed and feel they deserve it. Clearly, our princess is not going to allow herself to become one of those, although I can think of plenty of young women who have gone down this sad, passive route.

Once we ask for what we want, we are starting to love ourselves sufficiently that we become worthy of real love in return. And once we do that we give the other person the opportunity to be the best possible version of him or her self—and that's a real gift. The way we love ourselves will tend to be the way others will love us. It's a profoundly important realization.

If we wish to look at the tale from the point of view of the six archetypes of personal growth, we can see that the princess goes through the six archetypes in the correct order. She starts as an Innocent, playing like a child. The trouble is that all does not go her way. First, she loses the ball, then her father tells her she has to grow up and be responsible for what she promises. So she feels alienated and resentful, but also as if she has to conform—which is the Orphan archetype. Fortunately, her resentment sets her to questioning what she's ordered to do, which is the Pilgrim archetype's challenge, and finally she contacts her anger when she throws the frog at the wall. At this point she is acting as a Warrior archetype, who has yet to meet with her opposite, the Lover, so they can join together as the completed Warrior-Lover archetype. Yet, as we've already seen, when she asserts her personal sense of self-love, she is declaring that she deserves to be loved. In that single action she asserts that she is lovable, and that brings the lover into existence. That's why the young couple sleep together in the tale. It's a way of conveying that they are now joined in a loving and harmonious way, especially after the earlier conflict.

So, when the carriage arrives the next day, magically appearing from the Frog-King's country, the lovers are literally ready to become a king and a queen. Symbolically, in terms of personal development, this signals that the finding of a real, loving, trusting relationship elevates both the lovers to the degree of Monarch archetype. The princess can trust her own judgment. She can keep her word. She can love. She's a different person from the entitled little kid with the golden ball, and she's ready to be part of a real relationship.

This accounts for five of the six archetypes. The sixth, interestingly, is in the part of the tale that almost always gets forgotten, right at the end. The Grimm version has that strange episode of the servant, faithful Henry, who has had iron bands placed around his heart to contain his grief at his master's transformation into a frog. Now, the bands burst apart with a loud noise, so loud that the prince thinks the carriage is about to break. Instead, the last lines of the tale tell us, "It was only the bands which were springing from the heart of faithful Henry because his master was set free and happy."

What this signals to the reader is that when two people are truly alert to what's going on in their lives, and are well matched to each other, they become an inspiration for anyone who is observing them—because that's what's happening for faithful Henry. He knows his master is happy, and that this is not just a marriage of convenience or because the young king is grateful. This is the Magician archetype in operation—others become inspired by what the Magician shows them, and they are, in their turn, set free.

The king's son, then, can also be seen as having gone through the archetypal stages. He's been an Orphan, an outcast. As a frog, he has dwelt in the deep waters and has had to think about those depths in himself, too. When he pursues the princess to the castle, he becomes a Pilgrim and goes on his own pilgrimage. When she throws him against the wall, he has to have faith that this will set him free—it might kill him, after all. He shows courage in this, the courage of the Warrior-Lover who will risk his life for what and whom he loves.

Perhaps more important still is that he's seen the princess as herself, not as her public persona responding to his presence as a king's son. He knows who she is, and he accepts her. We'll notice that neither figure gets a promotion in rank by marrying the other. They're both royalty already, so this is not about social position, nor about one being rewarded in terms of prestige. They each have found their equal. What a wonderful way to telegraph to us that they are going to be evenly matched as lovers and as life partners!

It would not be stretching things too far to see the arrival of the carriage with its eight white horses as part of this theme. Historically, wealthy people prided themselves on their carriage horses and on the way the team was evenly paired and harmoniously matched, all working together to make the carriage travel efficiently. The carriage, therefore, is an emblem of harmony, befitting a young royal pair. The horses, we are told, are harnessed with "golden chains"—a suitable emblem of pairing in service to a higher cause, to responsibility, and the valuing of that responsibility. The symbolism suggests that both the princess and the king's son are at the Monarch archetype level, managing their carriage well in the same way as they will manage their kingdom and their own lives.

In this tale, both the king's son and the princess are allowed to achieve personal growth. They can't do it alone. They need each other. Similarly, for each of us, there are some aspects of spiritual growth that can't be done alone. They have to be experienced in a relationship. We discover most fully who we are when we're in relationship, not when we're isolated. We learn about love by loving.

The existence of faithful Henry, who had the iron hoops placed around his heart to prevent it from breaking when his master was first bewitched, is a clear indication to the readers that this prince can inspire love, respect, and loyalty—in fact, the exact same virtues that we expect to exist in the prince's marriage and in his future role as a king. This shows us he's worthy to be a king and that he's also worth marrying. This is why the ending of the tale actually does matter for our overall understanding of its meaning. If we've understood the symbolism we can see that this pair of lovers work as Magicians, inspiring faithful Henry—and us—with an enhanced sense of what love can be.

This, obviously, is not a trivial fairy tale. It's the first tale in the Grimm brothers' collection, and it starts them off on a suitably strong footing. It's never easy to describe psychosexual maturation in ways that are accessible and empowering, yet this story certainly seems to be doing this. It also taps into some very ancient ideas, since the frog had been seen as a symbol of sex and regeneration for centuries.

Frogs, as we know, go through several changes during their lifespans, from the white spawn found in ponds every spring, to the water-dwelling tadpole, to the air-breathing amphibian. Frogs have been used to symbolize change and regeneration since ancient times: they appear in the wall paintings of Çatal Hüyük, painted in 5,000 B.C. (I might also add that civilization has always placed a strong emphasis on the sacredness of wells, which is where this particular frog lives.)[1] So frogs do, indeed, have a long lineage as symbols; however, for our purposes in considering this tale, the obvious ability of the frog to change is what's important here, since that's what readers and listeners at the time would have identified first.

The frog also serves another purpose, since his transformation into a prince suggests the change that comes over adolescent girls when they first become interested in boys. Until that point they may have perceived boys as ugly and dirty, even froglike. When the hormones begin to do their work this attitude changes. This alteration is true of boys, also, who may think girls are silly and a waste of time—until puberty upends their attitude. The frog, the obvious symbol of change, operates on several levels to show us how sexual attraction can change everything seemingly overnight.

As mentioned earlier, the cliché of our times about "kissing a lot of frogs" derives from the Walt Disney version of this tale. The problem is that this inaccurate version removes the one strong action—the hurling of the frog against the wall—thereby taking all the power out of the tale. We're left with a dumb, weak-willed princess who gets a reward for no reason we can justify. The Grimm brothers' version surely has more resonance, which is why it deserves to be cherished.

Disneyfied fairy tales have a way of losing energy and relevance because they often miss the point. Worse still, perhaps, is that women I've spoken with have talked about "kissing a lot of frogs" as if this is a necessary part of the process of finding one's life partner. This is the way a cliché can take on a life of its own and become dangerous. What these women are saying, in effect, is that it is necessary to have a large number of unsatisfactory relationships with manipulative creeps before one can find a real man. Anyone who says that is truly asking for trouble and for misery. It's a really dangerous message to tell yourself, and it doesn't reflect the tale at all.

The princess, we'll notice, just has to have one "relationship" before she works out what she needs. A successful love life does not depend upon making a lot of mistakes that we know at the time are mistakes but hope might magically turn around and become something better. Acting like that is not only illogical, it's crazy. A successful emotional life means respecting ourselves, asking for what we want and need, then making sure we get it. We can't start to do that too soon, and there's no point in kissing a lot of amphibians if we don't actually want amphibians in our life. That's the power of metaphor. We have to see the pattern, not the concrete details. Reading the wrong tale too literally will leave you in bed with a creep every time.

If we turn our attention to the pattern, then, what we see is that the princess has good self-esteem at the start, but then she temporarily feels lost, and she finds herself again when she reestablishes her sense of personal value. To that extent she's just like any young woman growing up. She's fine with her usual comfortable world, but when boys come into the picture she may feel uncertain, and in this case she is abandoned by the one strong male figure she has—her father. This leaves her alone with her own emotions, which, for a while, she may distrust. That's why her anger is so important. It arises spontaneously, and she does not suppress it. She's back in touch with her authentic self. A real relationship has to be based on personal authenticity.

This is what we need to consider when we think of these tales as healing tales. In "The Frog-King," we see a natural process: in this case, the business of growing up and the challenges it produces. But the tale also offers the solution: we must get back in tune with our real feelings, for they will lead us to where we need to be. It is a healing tale for the confusions anyone can face when confronting possible suitors.

## CHAPTER 2

# "Faithful John"

## A Story of Parents, Jealousy, and Pride

One of the most overlooked of the Grimm brother's tales is "Faithful John," even though, as Tale No. 6. it occurs right at the start of the collection. It's a tale that sketches out in a masterful fashion the way a parent-child relationship could be, and the likely barriers to this. In the tale, a king is dying. He tells Faithful John, his servant, that the heir apparent should have access to every part of the castle but not to a certain locked room, which contains a portrait. The king fears that his son will see the portrait, fall in love with it, "fall in a swoon," and be in great danger.

It's indeed a fascinating tale, but one that can only be understood if seen as a very high form of metaphor—one in which almost everything has a spiritual value beyond the surface values. Here is the synopsis of the tale as it appears in Grimm.

The dying king asks Faithful John to be a "foster-father" to his son but to prevent the son from seeing the picture, which depicts the "Princess of the Golden Dwelling." Of course, following the king's death, when he is being shown around that castle, the young man asks for the locked room to be opened. Since the son is the king now, Faithful John has to obey. The young man sees the picture and swoons, desperately in love with the princess in the portrait.

The young king seems likely to die, so Faithful John comes up with a plan to take all the kingdom's gold and put it on a ship. Then, when they reach the Princess of the Golden Dwelling's land, Faithful John will pretend he's a merchant, take a few beautifully worked gold items to this princess who loves gold so much, show them to her, and then lure her aboard the ship with the promise of more. Once she is aboard, the ship will set sail.

They arrive in the princess's homeland, and Faithful John goes ashore disguised as a merchant. He speaks to a young woman carrying golden buckets of water and gains an audience with the princess. She sees the beautifully made items and agrees to visit the ship to see some more. All works out as planned, and the ship slips its cables and heads back with the kidnapped princess. Once he has her alone the young king declares his love, and after her initial shock wears off she agrees to marry him.

Things seem to be working out well. Then, one day, as Faithful John is sitting on deck, he hears three ravens speak.

One raven says that when the ship reaches shore a fine chestnut horse will appear, the king will mount it, and it will run off and fly into the air and he'll "never see his maiden more." The raven says that the only way this can be prevented is if someone jumps on the horse first and shoots it dead. Anyone who tells the king about all this will be turned to stone, from the feet to the knees.

The second raven says, in a rather mournful fashion, that it doesn't matter because, when the king gets to the castle, there will be a wedding garment waiting for him in a great dish, he'll put it on, and discover that it's not silver and gold but sulphur and pitch, which will burn and kill him. The only cure is if someone takes the dish and the clothing before he can put it on and tips the clothes into the fire. But, again, if anyone tells the king what's going on then that person will turn into stone from the knees to the heart.

The third raven, even more gloomy than the other two, says that during the wedding the bride will faint. She can only be saved from death if someone can "draw three drops of blood from her right breast and spit them out again." The penalty for revealing this information is to be turned entirely into stone.

Faithful John does not waver in his commitment to protecting the young king. Soon after the ship arrives in port, he sees the horse, jumps on it, draws his pistol, and kills it. The king does not complain or question this because, after all, Faithful John has always been faithful. Then, at the castle, Faithful John snatches the wedding garment from the king and tips it into the fire. Again the king is puzzled, but he says nothing. When the bride faints, though, and Faithful John draws three drops of blood from her right breast and spits them out, the young king loses his patience.

Faithful John is tried and condemned because he cannot say anything without being turned to stone. On the gallows he explains his actions but, of course, is turned into stone the moment he has finished. The young king laments the loss of his best servant and has the stone image brought into his bedroom.

One day, as the king is sorrowing over his servant's death, the statue speaks and says it can be restored to life if the king will cut off the heads of his twin boys who are playing nearby. Without hesitation he does this, and Faithful John immediately comes back to life. Then he puts the heads back on the boys, rubs the wounds with some blood, and they are restored to life as if nothing had happened.

The king hears the queen coming. He puts Faithful John and his boys into a cupboard and asks her where she has been. She's been praying for Faithful John, she says, wishing he would come back to life. The king then says this would be possible if she would agree to behead her two sons. Terrified, she says that she will agree, because "we owe it to him, for his great fidelity." When she says this, the king opens the cupboard and shows her the three all happily alive, and great joy is felt by all.

It's an unusual tale, there's no doubt about it, but contained within it are some meanings that are worth the effort of excavating.

The dying king obviously wants to protect his son from danger—in this case, the danger of erotic fascination with the princess. So we can begin this tale by seeing Faithful John as a father-substitute. This is helpful, since Faithful John must play the role of a father without the already existing emotional baggage that comes with the job of being a biological parent.

We're left asking why the dying king has a picture of this princess. Is this just a way to get the plot started, or do we infer that the dying king knows only too well what the disruptive power of love can feel like because he's felt it himself? He certainly knows his son, because the young man does, in fact, fall in a swoon when he sees the portrait, exactly as predicted. At this point we could say that this is mere infatuation and leave it at that. But notice: when the young king demands that the door be opened to him, he says that he will not be put off and that not looking inside the room will be his "certain destruction."

These are strong words. This is a person who will not be passive, who has tremendous drive, and is not about to give in to his servant. This is a leader. The question that arises, then, is to what extent does each generation fall in with the wishes of the previous generations? At what point is it necessary to go beyond what others have declared is good for us? The young king is emblematic of us all as we deal with this. If he'd just agreed not to look into the room because his faithful servant told him not to, what sort of king would he be?

But the tale has more for us. Faced with finding a solution to his young master's condition, it is Faithful John who hatches the plot to have the young king take all the gold in his treasury and have it turned into beautiful objects in order to charm the princess. He does so because the young king has declared he will give his life for her—and Faithful John is always careful to protect his monarch. We notice that there are several occasions in this tale when people have declared they'll do something or die in the attempt. We are not dealing with slight motivations here.

And that may cause us to think about the gold. It's tempting to see the gold, and the emphasis on it, as simply a way to make the tale seem more exotic and enhance the regard we have for the princess's status. But this would be to miss the point. Gold has always been held in high regard because it does not rust or corrode in any way. It is therefore a symbol of eternity. The young king is willing to give all he has (all his gold) to win the princess. Gold, then, can be seen not just as money but as an eternal value attached to the feelings the young king has for this woman. This is the power of love. She represents the eternal unfading nature of real love—not just passing erotic fancy.

The young king is expressing to us something very important about the nature of real emotion. When it arrives, it knocks us sideways and demands we do something about it, no matter what the cost might be. At this point, the king needs a father figure to guide him, and Faithful John steps in to offer fatherly advice without having to be fatherlike. In helping his young king's romantic hopes Faithful John displays a huge amount of self-sacrifice and love. In so doing, he assumes the role of father that a real-life father really should be able to take on for his sons, but so seldom manages to achieve. The tale's wisdom is that it displaces that emotionally charged role onto a more neutral figure—and, in the process, shows fathers everywhere how they could operate in their sons' lives.

At the princess's castle, Faithful John first sees the beautiful maiden with the golden water buckets before he talks to the princess herself. By pretending to be a merchant, he gets to see people as they really are, not as their public persona. The maiden he encounters first is respectful and does the right thing—she takes him to the princess right away.

Notice that the maiden is carrying two golden buckets of water. It's an odd detail, but it signals something. The first is that she's doing her job in a well-run kingdom. Every castle needs a supply of water. The second implication is that gold is beautiful (as she is) but that, ultimately, everyday life has to happen. Water can be carried resentfully by grubby peasants using dirty wooden buckets, or it can be carried by beautiful maids with golden buckets. It still has to be delivered. The unusual use of the gold lets us know this kingdom is not about money or ostentation; it's about harmony, beauty, and a loving connection between ruler and subject. If it were anything else, the maid would be leaving, fast, with the golden buckets in a sack over her shoulder.

The princess is then lured aboard the boat and kidnapped. This is a troublesome action. After all, she's been open and trusting compared with Faithful John who has been devious, albeit in service to his king.

Once again, we need to see this action in a different, symbolic way. By bringing all his gold along with him on board ship, the young king is doing the equivalent of bringing all his finest emotional resources to the princess, without holding anything back. When she sees the extent of his love, eventually the princess is happy to accept the young king as her husband.

Seen realistically this explanation is nonsense; however, if we look at it symbolically, we can say that the young king understands the princess deeply, through her love of the beauty and purity of gold, and he responds to that. We could say that he knows her and what she cares about, and in this instance it's not the value of the gold but the purity of spirit that it conveys. That is what the maid with the golden buckets conveys, also.

For her part, the princess notices that she is loved and witnesses the kind of man the young king is—one who understands her and honors his own emotions. Certainly, it's a code, but it indicates enough for us to see that there is a deeper sympathy than mere passing fancy at issue; there's a reciprocity that makes the young king and princess equals. Notice, too, that the king has been on a voyage, and by kidnapping the princess she is now taken on a voyage. Each has left home territory and is prepared to venture all they have for the other.

It is at this point that Faithful John overhears the ravens. We notice that the ravens foretell the future, so they may be linked to the Three Fates of antiquity; however, these ravens are quite explicit about what will happen. The large chestnut horse will have to be killed (the pistol is an anachronism of the eighteenth century), and anyone who attempts to tell the young king about this creature will be turned to stone from the toes to the knees—a fitting punishment of immobility, since the horse is a symbol of mobility, as well as power, energy, and, above all, pride in being able to display that mobility. The young king must be saved from the pride of personal display that the horse represents.

The wedding garment—which has to be taken away and burned—can, therefore, be seen as an emblem of the pride of being special on a special day. This garment, like the shirt of Nessus that Hercules was forced to endure and which drove him mad, must be destroyed, so that the young king's pride does not overwhelm him.[1] Fittingly, the punishment for attempting to explain this is to be turned to stone from the knees to the heart—an area covering the genitals and the very organ in which emotion is located: the heart. The entire feeling part of the body will be forfeit. Notice also that the wedding garment will cover most of the body, from the neck down to about knee level, and so there is once again a correspondence between the symbolic object and the part of Faithful John that will be turned to stone.

The third prediction is that the princess will fall down in a swoon and Faithful John will have to take three drops of blood from her breast and spit them out. Notice that it is now the princess's turn to swoon, and she does so during the dance. Dancing, especially in the ritual of the bride and groom taking the first dance at a wedding, is an emblem of their ability to be with each other harmoniously, to be "in step" with each other. The fact that the princess swoons and has to be saved by Faithful John parallels what happened to the young king, and to some extent it shows the princess as being as in love with the king as he is with her. They are, one might say, overcome with the sense of what their love can be.

Alas, Faithful John's actions may save the day, but he is forced to speak about why he did what he did and is promptly turned to stone, just as the ravens predicted. It's an odd action, though, taking three drops of blood from the princess's right breast, presumably by biting her; we may understand it better if we see the three actions of Faithful John as his way of once again shielding the young king.

As we've already noticed, the killing of the horse can be seen as the removal of the lure of the vanity of superiority, which he takes away from the young king. Fine horses are items in which the wealthy take considerable pride to this day, and a king's horse is always a source of prestige. Being able to control a spirited horse is a metaphor—the good ruler has a spirited horse that he can control in the same way as he is expected to keep a lively kingdom in check. We have only to look at royal portraits in museums and galleries to see how often kings are depicted seated on fiery, snorting horses that contribute to the monarch's glamour.

Faithful John removes the temptation of public ostentation, so that the young king will remain "grounded." Remember: the ravens tell Faithful John that the horse will fly away. It is a fitting emblem of the intoxication of power—ask any teenager who has zoomed his parents' car to a heavy speeding fine.

The same series of values is true of the clothing. The wedding garment's destruction can be seen as Faithful John's intervention to remove the shallow pride of appearances, which can waylay any young and powerful person. Monarchs from George IV of England to "mad" Prince Ludwig of Bavaria have reveled in fine clothing—at the expense of paying attention to their kingdoms. Faithful John's actions can be seen, therefore, as removing the temptation of private pride and self-aggrandizement.

But the drawing of blood? This is less obvious and more suggestive. By his actions, Faithful John shows that the princess is just a physical woman, not a spirit or a goddess to be revered or worshipped. She's flesh and blood; and the blood isn't anything special, either—it gets spat out. The event seems arranged to highlight the way young lovers tend to idealize the loved one and become overly attached to the sensual joys of sex—which will, to some extent, fade over time. The young king could easily fall into this way of thinking and forget that he's married to a woman of flesh and blood.

Seen this way the three tests are specifically designed for the education of the young king. He needs a father figure who is dedicated to his well-being to tell him that racing around on fine horses is not important, nor is pomp and ceremony, while physical and sexual indulgence—with its negative trait of possessiveness—is not to be taken to an extreme, either. The young king is prevented from three potentially addictive traps. Real love is not about having the trophy spouse, nor is it about the fine appearance one may make in the world, and it certainly goes far deeper than the splendid sex life that, inevitably, has to alter as the couple grows older and children appear.

Such are the illusions of marriage. We know this all too well in our world, where wealthy and influential males tend to divorce one wife and then marry another who looks very similar to the first bride, but who just happens to be twenty years younger. They don't seem to be able to face the reality of growing old with an actual person, and so they opt for the delusion of perpetual youth.

This is a cliché of our times, and it tells us that the lessons in this fairy-tale have not been learned as well as we might wish by the world at large. It also tells us that these lessons are, perhaps, best imparted by a father figure, one who is not afraid to look foolish or risk being misunderstood. Some insights, especially those about the nature of love, are too important to remain undelivered. Certainly, from marriages and divorces I have observed, I could only wish that these lessons had been delivered more regularly.

Faithful John, though, suffers. An important element here is that, in telling his reasons for doing as he did, he is turned to stone. This prevents the young king from having to punish him, and it also invites us to see that the king was ready to condemn his servant because of the blow to his personal pride. He was personally outraged that his servant dared to suck blood from his new bride's breast, and he did not stop to consider that this might be for reasons he did not know anything about.

The stone figure of Faithful John is then moved into the bedroom. If we had any doubt at all that this tale was about love, sex, and fidelity, this would be the moment we'd have no question as to its tendency. In time, the princess gives birth to twin boys, which the king then has to sacrifice to bring Faithful John back to life.

The twins are an interesting detail. It shows us that, since Faithful John has saved both his master's life and the life of the princess, two lives are now his to claim. By concealing the twins and Faithful John in a cupboard and asking the princess to agree to sacrifice her children, both the king and his queen are each independently given the opportunity to agree that they have a debt to Faithful John, and then to pay it willingly.

This part of the story is problematic for many readers. It looks as if it's been tacked on. Yet it seems to match the tale thematically, so we have to ask what it is trying to say in a thematic sense. In some ways this is alarmingly obvious: a father and mother should not ignore the call to do what is morally right, even though it may seem to cost them their family. Doing what is right is more important than doing what seems to be comfortable, especially in the case of a ruling monarch.

While the apparent sacrifice of children may appear repugnant to our modern age—indeed any age—we must remind ourselves that this is *not* a realistic tale about what we do every day. It's not a how-to manual of parenting; it's a metaphor. As such, it seems to indicate that if we allow our moral obligations to a parent figure to go unrecognized—if we fail to see what our parents and elders did for us, and how we didn't understand some of their actions at the time—then the whispering voice of doubt will haunt the bedroom until we do acknowledge that they may have had some wisdom.

We need to be able to let our parents' wisdom back into our lives, even though we may have rejected their views at the time. Perhaps we harbor resentments about our parent's actions and the way they treated us when we were in love. Perhaps we were wrong about some of those resentments. The lesson is surprisingly simple: we can't love our spouse and children fully without at some point coming to terms with how we misunderstood our parents, when all they wanted to do was to protect us and guide us.

The tale, therefore, offers a vitally important life lesson, especially since the young king has become a parent himself and is about to face those exact same challenges. Both he and the princess need to see that there are some things one has to do that may, at first, seem to harm the children. Cosseting them will not do them any good; sometimes one really does have to be cruel to be kind.

This reminds us of the dying king at the start of the story. If he had one fault it was that he wished to protect his son and preserve his life, no matter what. He imagined the Princess of the Golden Dwelling was the problem, when, in actual fact, *he* was the problem. The wish to save one's child from having to learn the hard way is foremost in any parent's mind. Unfortunately it can give rise to overly protective parenting and is still commonplace today. The dying king obviously felt that passionate love was more dangerous than his son could bear. He himself had ordered the portrait to be locked away, so he cannot have ever allowed himself to pursue that kind of love. His own fear about love, therefore, has made him doubt his son's capacity. He means well, but he would rather his son lived a tame, half-lived life than take a risk and achieve real happiness. In this tale, the young king and his wife have to learn that clinging to their children will not work this time; then, when their children are magically healed, we can interpret that as a kind of rebirth of their parents' relationship to them.

Perhaps the best way to describe this situation is to consider the parent who will not discipline a child. It may be because that parent is so caught up in being special for the child, or being the child's best friend, or is afraid of not being a good parent, that the parent cannot bear to risk that relationship by being stern. No matter the reason, the parent is afraid to criticize the child, and the correction does not occur.

One can almost hear the ancestors rolling over in their tombs—just as the voice of Faithful John echoes in the bedchamber.

The tale, then, is not about the children being killed; instead, it's about them not being indulged or made precious at the expense of principles. The young king and his spouse don't love their twins any less afterward; they simply don't see them the same way. At the end of the tale, the young king sees Faithful John alive again and says: "God be praised, he is delivered; and we have our little sons again, also." Notice the sons come second.

Another parent-child relationship example may be helpful here. I can think of at least one instance where a parent routinely allowed a very young child to ride in the front seat of the family car without using a seat belt. This, as we know, is very unwise. When I questioned the mother about this, she replied that the child wanted to ride in the front and didn't like seat belts. Then, she recalled—and this is the most interesting part—that when she was a child she hated being told to use her seat belt, so now she was a parent she wasn't going to do that to her child. She was entirely closed to reasonable discussion on the topic.

What had happened here was that the mother had had such a strong visceral reaction to her own parents' way of doing things that she'd created a potentially disastrous situation. She was, of course, entitled to her own feelings and reactions; however, she was not entitled to put someone else at risk because of those feelings.

I have plenty of sympathy with this reaction, but only up to a point. In my own life, I have frequently found myself feeling that I must sound just like my father when I insist on my passengers, especially children, using their seat belts; but I know I have to do it anyway. At such times I think of Faithful John, whispering his good advice, and try and listen for it.

The entire story, then, can be seen as a highly complex and suggestive tale that asks the reader to consider the roles of parents with their children, especially in terms of the wish to be over-protective. The dying king could not have helped his son to find real love because he was obviously afraid of its power. That's why he locks the portrait away. Fortunately Faithful John can give the necessary advice and be heard, at least some of the time. Which of us hasn't disregarded a parent's advice simply because it came from that parent? Yet when the guidance comes from a parent substitute, we can often hear it loud and clear.

Faithful John, turned to stone and placed in the bedroom, is brought back to life by being loved and because his advice is heard, no matter how bizarre that advice might seem. One could say that when he is a statue he's an apt image for those parents who are cut out of their children's lives because of some misunderstanding that has derailed the relationship. As I grow older, I continually recognize that many of the things my parents did that annoyed me so much at the time were probably meant for my own good and showed considerable insight; I just couldn't see it at the time. As we know, in so many cases, it is the arrival of grandchildren that allows the whole parental dynamic to be rethought by all concerned, and healed. And that's just what we see in the tale. By no means does it say that we ought to give in to our parents at all times; however, it does ask us to rethink that relationship and see it in a new way.

In terms of the six archetypes of personal and spiritual growth, the tale is remarkably clear. The dying king wants to keep his son as an Innocent, or possibly as an Orphan, following the rules even after he is dead. The young king has no patience with that. When he orders Faithful John to open the locked door, he is refusing the cozy "adoption" of conforming to what everyone, especially his father, expects.

He's an explorer—a Pilgrim—and, as his sea voyage with the gold shows, one who is ready to take a risk for what he believes in. When he is accepted by the princess, he is ready to be a Warrior-Lover, one who has fought for what he wants and who can now love her because she is worthy of the efforts he has invested in her. The princess also seems to see these qualities in him, for she accepts his love without too much trouble. She's already shown herself as a capable princess in her own land, so she is an equal match for the young king.

As a king who accepts what Faithful John does, no matter how odd, the young king is the Monarch archetype, prepared to extend trust to those whom he knows are worthy of it. But he reaches his limit when Faithful John sucks blood from his bride's breast. His pride has been injured. He's jealous, and the ego basis of personal pride is a powerful and often corrosive force that threatens all of us. To some extent his placing of the statue of Faithful John in the bedroom is his acknowledgment that he allowed his emotions to get the better of him: by placing the statue in such a personal and sexual space, we can see that he feels this personally as what it truly is— sexual jealousy that is unworthy of a king. This odd choice of bedroom furniture suggests that this is not just a vague public apology; it's a heartfelt daily reminder. He doubted the faith of his servant and, by association, he doubted the fidelity of his bride, too.

It is not until the young king credits what he alone hears (Faithful John's voice from the statue), and takes steps to act upon what he believes, that he becomes a real Magician. The magic derives from the fact that the children are healed, and by implication the next generation is made whole. This can only happen because the young king has total faith in what he is doing and total trust in the wisdom of the directions.

Sometimes, what is rational and explicable is not the correct way forward. Sometimes, we have to grab our sense of faith and act as we feel. In this sense, the ending of the tale is not unlike the Biblical story of Abraham and Isaac, where Abraham is told to sacrifice his only son, Isaac, on an altar. He obeys this command, even though he feels his heart will break. As we'll recall, at the last moment God provides a substitute in the form of a ram, thus saving Isaac.[2]

The Biblical echo in the Grimm brothers' tale cannot be accidental. In Abraham's case, the faith being tested is his faith in God; for the young king, it is faith in his servant. We have to remember, however, that this is a servant who can hear and understand the speech of ravens, so he is, at least in part, a sort of Magician, in tune with nature, including human nature. Faithful John never doubts what he has to do, nor asks why. This is what the young king has to learn—to trust the inner voice.

We could choose to see this situation in our everyday world as the person who, in his private chamber, in the privacy of his own mind, recalls some piece of advice given to him by a wise parental figure about the nature of his relationship. At that point he can choose to shut out this wisdom because it may not be quite what he wishes it to be, or he can choose to act on it. If he does, the tale says, it will be a personal decision; indeed, it must be.

Notice that it's only after he's beheaded the children, has had them brought back to life, and restored Faithful John that the king asks the queen if she'll agree to do what he's already done. And she does.

If we translate this into modern terms, sometimes parents have to be firm in handling children (especially twin boys, as in this tale!). This toughness has to come from personal choice and conviction that this is the best way forward. If it comes from some sort of patched-up agreement between the parents, then there is plenty of room for the child to manipulate the weaker parent and undermine the decision.

It could be a case of "Mom says I can't go, but if I ask Dad he almost always agrees" (or the reverse). Or perhaps the decisive parent might say that little Suzy has to go to camp this summer because it'll be good for her, and the other, softer, parent says, after Suzy's been there a whole day, that the child is obviously homesick and they should bring her back.

In the tale both the king and queen independently come to the same conclusion as to what has to be done, and not because one persuades the other or talks the other round. The parents are united in decisive action, and each is certain the action is the best thing. There is much wisdom to be gained from this.

This trusting of the inner voice, symbolized by Faithful John's whisper in the bedroom, is lacking in many of our lives. The person who hates her job but doesn't leave it because everyone will think it doesn't make sense—this is someone who is not prepared to respect the inner voice. The parent who agrees to have her teenager go to what she knows is a questionable party because everyone else seems to be allowing it is in the same situation. Interestingly, when a parent disciplines a child, young people still sometimes refer to it as "having their heads bitten off." A good telling-off is sometimes necessary, and no one dies from it.

If the tale defies easy categorization and glib endings, then it is because it paints a picture rather than explains with words. We are asked to see how the world is, not to analyze it. In this, we are like the characters in the story.

So, what is the story telling us? It shows us that when young men fall in love, they will need the guidance of their fathers; however, in order to do this, the father must step into a different role—that of adviser rather than director. Under these circumstances the adviser requires trust, not to be questioned in all that he does, since explaining leads to a deadening of the relationship—symbolized by turning into stone. That troublesome scene in which the young king cuts off the heads of his twins is simply the most extreme and dramatic representation of what is required in terms of trust. It's a metaphor. The young, even when they love truly and with great boldness, still need directing, and the wisdom of others deserves respect, so that the joyous ending can occur.

When stated like this, it may sound simple; yet, I am sure we can all think of far more families in which the old and faithful relatives are disrespected and their wisdom ignored than we can recall families where there is harmony and real trust. Perhaps Mark Twain put it best when he said: "When I was a boy of fourteen, my father was so ignorant I could hardly stand to have the old man around. But when I got to twenty-one, I was astonished at how much the old man had learned in seven years."[3]

The Magician archetype is revealed in the harmony of the closing scene. When parents act out of sound principles and wisdom and allow themselves to recognize good advice from their own elders, then good things happen. This is not always the case, though—as the tale lets us know. Remember, the young king ignores his father's dying directive not to open the locked door. The directive, as we've seen, is not a good one, and the young king could have used that incident and the whole successful episode of his marriage voyage to point to that one disobedience and use it to justify some future willfulness. This is why, at the end of the tale, he needs to be seen to be open to real, good advice and able to trust it. It's in that trust and balance that the healing occurs.

The tale doesn't tell us how to live our lives; it doesn't give directives. It asks us, instead, to be aware of the tensions that gather around the issue of trusting one's elders in the tale of a young man growing into personal autonomy.

This brings us back to the important detail of Faithful John turning into stone, which we can now understand with greater clarity. We've already noticed how the parts of the body that will be turned into stone by anyone who tells the young king about the prophecy correspond to the "test" that each event creates. The horse prediction, as a representation of mobility, will cause the feet to be turned to stone; the wedding garment, as a symbol of sexual pride, will cause the same thing to happen to the body at the level of the genitals and heart; and the biting of the bride's breast, with the possessiveness and suspicion that comes with it, will cause the head as the source of reason to be turned to stone, too. There is perfect coherence in these symbols.

Yet, there is another layer of meaning available to us. If Faithful John simply removes the tests from the young king he can remain human, but if he *tells* anyone why he does this he suffers the fate of turning into stone. The hint is very strong—when a father figure unilaterally declares what has to be done, *telling* his children what to do, then he takes the risk of being seen merely as someone who forbids, as a monolithic force as immovable as stone.

For generations, children have dehumanized their parents, smarting from restrictions they do not understand and which have not been explained to them. Parents and authority figures are sometimes seen by the child as stone-faced, unyielding, and unapproachable. Yet if one tries to reason with a child and explain why something isn't good for her, there is always an occasion when the child just doesn't want to understand, no matter what age he or she is! Sometimes, the parent just has to make an executive decision, without explanation. Enough candy is enough candy; sometimes one just has to take the car keys away, or say "no." On such occasions, detailed explanations aren't always helpful.

In fact, the tale hints that no matter what course of action parents take, at some stage it is going to be their fate to be seen as unyielding, just as Faithful John finds himself turned into a statue. The tale reminds us that families don't run smoothly. There are deadlocks, but they can be overcome. It's excellent advice for anyone when we don't want to listen to reason—most of us are part of a family and may tend to close our hearts when we don't get our own way and don't understand why. The tale asks us to bear this in mind, so we can keep our hearts open.

Faithful John is that rarest of individuals, a father figure who knows when to hand power back to the son. The aim is not, as we see in so many families, for the senior person to hang onto power and influence as long as possible. The aim is to help empower the next generation by stepping back in a timely manner, allowing them to be "kings" and be in charge of their own lives, intruding as little as possible. This is what allows independence to grow. It's a risky way forward, seemingly far more so than any other course of action. It is, however, more beneficial than the iron grip, maintained until death, which only infantilizes the next generation.

## CHAPTER 3

# "Brother and Sister"

### Boy and Girls Grow Up Differently and see Marriage Differently

Tale No. 11 in the Grimm brothers' collection is the unusual story called "Brother and Sister." We'll need to refresh our memories of the plot to understand it fully. In this tale, two children—the brother and sister in the title—run away from a wicked stepmother who is also a witch. As they run they become very thirsty, but the witch has placed a spell on the streams. The first stream mutters a warning that only the sister can hear—anyone who drinks from it will be turned into a tiger. Afraid that her brother will become a tiger and devour her, the girl warns him away from the stream, and they walk on. The next stream also issues a warning, except that this time the message is that anyone who drinks from it will be turned into a wolf; again, the sister hears it and warns her brother. The third stream warns that anyone drinking from it will be turned into a roebuck. This time, though, the brother is so thirsty he drinks anyway and is promptly turned into a deer. The sister takes off her "golden garter" and places it round her brother's neck, then makes a rope of reeds and leads him around so he will not run away.

The sister and her brother, the roebuck, find a house in the woods. They live there until, one day, the roebuck hears the sound of the hunt and cannot bear not to run off and join in. The sister allows this on condition that, when he returns, he'll announce himself at the door, which she will have barred for safety, using the words: "Little sister, let me in."

On the first day the brother returns safely, although the huntsmen have been much interested by this beautiful buck with the golden collar. On the next day he is slightly wounded but makes it home safely. He has, however, been followed by a huntsman who hears the password and reports back to the king. On the third day the king goes to the hut, uses the password before the buck returns, meets the sister, and asks her to marry him. All three then go off to live in his castle, and the sister gives birth to a child a year later.

Meanwhile, the wicked stepmother has found out the whereabouts of the step-daughter and decides her ugly one-eyed daughter should have been queen rather than her stepsister. Mother and daughter head off to the castle and tell the still weak sister that she should take a bath. The stepmother makes the fire to heat the water so intensely hot the sister is overcome, suffocates, and dies. The stepmother then makes the ugly stepsister look almost like the dead sister by using spells and tells her to get into the king's bed.

At first it looks as if the ruse has been successful. Then, at midnight, the dead sister returns, feeds her infant and strokes her brother, the roebuck, and departs. The nurse is too frightened to do anything, although she does tell the king. The king watches the second night, but we are told that he "dared not speak" to his dead wife when she appears. The third night he watches again, speaks to her, and she is brought back to life.

The scheming witch and her ugly daughter are found out. As punishment, the ugly daughter is torn to pieces by wild creatures—an interesting reprise of the fears of the young sister when she and her brother were lost in the woods. In a similar echo the witch is punished by being burned, which reminds us of the young mother's death in the over-heated bathroom. Finally, with the death of the witch, the brother is released from the spell that has been cast upon him and becomes human again.

It's worth going into this plot in such detail because we see right away that there are several formal elements of organization. There are three streams, three days of the hunt, and three nights during which the dead queen appears. The fate of the witch and her daughter parallels the fears and experience of the sister. So the question arises as to what this tale means.

To some extent, it is fairly clearly a tale about how girls grow up. The sister knows she needs her brother, and she's clearly less impulsive than he is, or he'd have drunk from the first stream. As children grow up there is a tendency for them to fight and assert themselves against each other, and the boy, as a tiger or a wolf, would certainly have been only interested in his own survival, not hers.

We have, therefore, a suggestion about the sort of boy-girl sibling rivalry we can witness in any family, and the sister to some degree controls her brother for his own good. When he is turned into a roebuck, though, he ceases to be of any use at all, and she even has to restrain him from his impulse to run away by using the golden garter. As a portrait of the scattered nature of some children, it works well. Boys in early adolescence have a tendency to "run wild" and to run into danger. Unfortunately, the sister cannot protect him forever—and eventually, he feels he has to go off and participate in the hunt, even though the hunt is focused on him!

The sister knows the hunt signifies danger for her brother (as when a boy today might wish to engage in dangerous sports), and she knows it'll be dangerous for her, too. Huntsmen will be in the woods, so her door must be barred. If we needed further confirmation of her sexual fears, we have only to recall that the Roman goddess of sexual love, Venus, was also the goddess associated with hunting. "Venison," the name popularly given to deer meat, means "belonging to Venus," or "that which has been gained from the hunt." Since the brother is a deer, this is pretty clearly a connection we are supposed to make. The sister is, therefore, part of a drama that is obviously about sex and the thrill of the hunt.

And she is effectively hunted down by the king. What we notice, though, is that she obviously has self-control (unlike her brother) and some good solid common sense. Moreover, she recognizes that the king has fine qualities; he accepts that her brother, the roebuck, must come with her, and so he's not the sort of boor who would see the deer as merely a source of food.

When she gives birth and is killed, we could say that she is "replaced" by the one-eyed hag of a stepsister. If we wish to see this as a mythic transformation, we could also say that it mirrors the changes that can happen when women become mothers. For a while they are not the same sexually desirable creatures as they were before, since they're exhausted and involved with feeding and caring for the child. If the father is present at the birth, often the woman is perceived in that painful process as turning into something very other, and even can become frightening. Women have reported that, while in labor, they have cursed at and sworn at their husbands, blaming them for making them pregnant, and therefore forcing them to go through all this pain. The whole process can be a bit of a shock to some men. The sweet loving spouse has, temporarily, taken on the aspects of the hag.

Understanding this helps to explain the next section. The queen "dies" and reappears as a ghost, responsible and loving and caring for both her child and her brother. We could say that, in this way, the king gets to see her true loving spirit again, so he reclaims her as his wife. This is richly suggestive of the moment when, seeing his wife and newborn child together, the husband falls more deeply in love than ever before, and she with him. The temporary sense of alienation that many husbands feel when they see their wives wholly wrapped up in the newborn is replaced by something larger, more generous, and more deeply loving. In the tale, the king's action brings his wife back to life, and she "became fresh, rosy, and full of health."

Viewed in this light, the tale can be seen as a sensitive appreciation of the ways girls develop, as opposed to the ways boys develop, and that lasting love is based on more than simple attraction. It tells the alert reader what can happen when children arrive, and how that event can enrich, rather than threaten, the love bond.

If we look at the king for a moment, we could say that he moves from his very male activities of hunting toward a world of real affection. We can trace echoes of this when we see young men who are seemingly fully engaged in sports, spending their time with their male friends, all being lads together, then one of them is introduced to the sister of his friend, and suddenly romance is in the air. During the hunt, the king knows the roebuck is something special, and knowing this he is aware, perhaps, that his life search is for something more vital than just another set of antlers in his castle.

It's a sensitive tale, clearly, about boys and girls growing up, and about the transition of girls from sisters to lovers, then to mothers, and what that involves. In fact, we can choose to see the tale as a whole series of developments in archetypal terms.

The children start as complete Innocents and quickly become Orphans by running away. The girl is then seen as the responsible, cautious child: for her, the Pilgrim phase is the long, patient time she spends in the isolated house, tending her brother, learning about loving him and caring for him, even though he can contribute nothing to the household. Her determination to take him along to the king's palace is her recognition of the love bond of family, balanced with that bond she shares with her husband. They are different bonds, but one cannot be abandoned for the other.

We could say the sister learns the role of the Warrior-Lover, fighting for her survival and that of her beloved brother, before she finds its full expression in her marriage. She knows what love and devotion are, and so is ready for marriage. This, of course, turns her into a queen, so we could see the royal pair as being at the Monarch stage; yet, there is more for us to consider because there is a second part to her experience.

From her role as wife and lover, the sister gives birth and moves into her role as the nurturer of her child. When she is abducted and suffocated by her stepmother, she "dies" in a metaphorical sense because her old life will never be available for her again. Ask any parent about this. Many I know have referred to their lives B.C.—Before Children—with a whimsical sense that things can never return to those simple early days again. The sister is now a mother, and the added loving responsibility is a spiritual elevation: when the king sees her and reclaims her, he is not just rediscovering his love for her but claiming his love for her in their new role and in their new life together. In this role they are no longer the focus, so much as the next generation is. They are truly the guardians of the next generation, true Monarchs working together for the good of all.

When the king chooses this role—notice, he has to claim it; it's not just handed to him—everything changes. Once he's stepped forward, his wife reclaims him, too. They are, the tale seems to say, equals. This is when the final archetype, the Magician, occurs. The queen comes back to life, the wicked are punished, and the spell on the brother is dissolved.

When we see the tale in this way even the smallest details become important. So, for example, the fear that the brother may become a tiger if he drinks from the first stream, and a wolf if he drinks from the second, gestures at the way children can react when mistreated by parents. Their initial reaction may well be furious tigerlike anger, which they then take out on any available sibling, because they have no one else to take it out on. After some time has passed following the trauma, the reaction may be just as angry but less direct. Like a wolf, who lurks to see what he can steal, the child can become destructive in a less overt way. When the brother does finally drink he becomes a roebuck, irresponsible and skittish, almost to the point of self-destructiveness. From my experience with disturbed adolescents this seems like an accurate rendition of the way children can adopt an "I don't care" attitude when the mistreatment has happened some time before. This is just another expression of anger, transformed by the delay.

The compressed nature of this tale is particularly impressive. So much information appears in such a suggestive and thought-provoking way, we can only conclude that this tale would have been the starting point for all sorts of other discussions, by the readers and listeners, about the relationship of the sexes to each other. One of the roles of stories, after all, is to stimulate dialogue.

Interestingly, the next tale in the Grimm brothers' collection is "Rapunzel" (Tale No.12), another story that requires a password to be overheard, so that a young woman in an out-of-the-way building can meet the man who will propose to her. We'll recall that in the tale of "Rapunzel" the king's son overhears the Enchantress asking Rapunzel to let down her hair, and knowing this allows him to scale the tower.

The very next story in the sequence is "The Three Little Men in the Wood" (Tale No. 13), which shares some remarkable similarities with "Brother and Sister." As in the earlier tale, having successfully met her royal husband, the young queen is also surprised by her stepmother and ugly stepsister. Here, too, the queen has recently given birth and is killed—this time by being thrown into a stream. She reappears as a duck, then transforms herself into a ghost and visits her child three times before the king recognizes her. In both tales, the words of the spirit-queen (and the spirit-duck) are spoken in verse, which is an unusual feature.

The decision of the Grimm brothers to put such similar tales together serves several purposes. First, it shows us, relatively early on in the collection, that there will be many variants and repeated elements in these tales as we read them. A different sort of editor might have attempted to keep such similar tales as far apart as possible, in the hope that no one would notice the similarity. Instead, the Grimms' decision to group them in this way alerts us to the curious nature of the repetitions and leads us to make connections.

For example, we can see that in both "Brother and Sister" and in "The Three Little Men in the Wood," the queen is in a very weak state when her stepmother and stepsister arrive; in both stories, she takes a bath—either in a too-hot room or in a stream—that kills her, and in each case she is replaced by the ugly sister.

This may well be a way of suggesting that some women suffer a deeper transformation after childbirth, a form of postnatal depression, perhaps, which makes them temporarily into "ugly" versions of themselves. In "The Three Little Men in the Wood," the stepmother even tells the king not to go near the ugly sister, who is disguised as his wife in their bed, because she is in a "terrible sweat"—a clear indication of some sort of postnatal illness; in "Brother and Sister," the excuse is that the queen should not be allowed to see any light yet. These hints are strong enough to support the postnatal depression argument.

They may also indicate that taking a hot bath after giving birth is a good idea—not only from the point of view of hygiene but because, symbolically, it offers a form of baptism for the mother, a sort of renewal; and that if this is not done in a caring and loving way, the result will be psychically highly damaging. The newly delivered mother needs to be brought back to the ordinary world gently, and with compassion. It's an important message.

We also need to consider other plot similarities. In "Brother and Sister," we notice that the king has to claim his ghost queen as his wife. He announces, "You can be none other than my dear wife," and she claims him right back, confirming, "Yes, I am your dear wife." This wording is exactly the same as that used by the king when he first proposed ("Will you go with me to my palace and be my dear wife?" followed by her agreement), so we can make some suggestions as to the meaning.

The claim and counterclaim seem to act as a renewal of the original marriage agreement, signaling a return to the earlier state of sexual and emotional harmony. The marriage is alive again, by mutual consent, after a period of estrangement. In "The Three Little Men in the Wood," the king has to break the spell by waving his sword above the spirit-queen's head three times. The significance of a man waving a large phallic symbol above his bride's head—in the middle of the night, no less—cannot have gone unnoticed. He's reclaiming his wife, as well as their sex life.

Obviously this is intimate territory. As anyone who has become a parent will know, sometimes the resuming of sex between the parents can be a delicate matter. The woman may still be healing, and may even be afraid of further pregnancies. It's not something that can be rushed. Sometimes, in fact, both men and women lose sexual interest in each other when a child arrives. This is partly what lies behind this tale.

Even in modern times, postpartum ailments—both physical and emotional—are all too frequently disregarded. For example, actress Brooke Shields' recent statements about her experience of postnatal depression, revealed in her book *Down Came the Rain, My Journey Through Postpartum Depression* (Hyperion Books, 2005), were treated by some men, including actor Tom Cruise, with real disrespect. The amount of television time devoted to Ms. Shields and her response lets us know that this is a topic of vital importance to many, even though it is a borderline taboo subject and is widely misunderstood.

Viewed in this light, we can certainly claim that the tales of "Brother and Sister" and "The Three Little Men in the Wood" are conveying information that remains relevant to modern readers. The tales don't tell us in any overt way what we should do about these thorny issues; that is not their purpose. Instead, they let us know that these changes can happen and that they are not permanent, and that like so many emotional challenges, love is the answer.

## CHAPTER 4

# "The Three Spinners" and "Rapunzel"

## The Nature of the Tales and Thwarted Young Love

At this point we begin to notice something about the Grimm tales: they are easily divided into those tales in which characters grow and change and those tales in which no change occurs. For example, in "The Good Bargain" (Tale No. 7), the doltish peasant gains money but only through his own dumb luck. Likewise, in "The Three Spinners" (Tale No. 14), the lazy spinner is saved from her fate by a trick ending, and she hardly seems to deserve her luck, either.

The tale of "The Three Spinners," in brief, concerns a prince who is ready to marry a lazy spinner based entirely on her reputation as a good spinner; he then finds out that, in fact, the spinning has all been done by her three ugly "aunts," who have appeared magically. When he asks how they got to be so ugly, the three women say it was from the three repeated actions required in spinning yarn. Working the treadle caused one to have a huge foot, licking the thread caused the second to have a big lip, and twisting the thread caused the last one to have an enormous thumb. The prince, horrified that his wife might be affected the same way, forbids her to spin ever again. End of problem.

These kinds of stories are closer to the sort of things we'd recognize today as extended jokes, with a punchline that solves the premise but in a ridiculous way. This is not to say that the story of the lazy spinner is without merit. To gain insight into the way the world works, we have only to notice that the plot makes some specific points about the roles of women.

Let's look at the plot in its entirety.

The lazy girl at the center of the story hates to spin yarn, incurring the anger of her mother, who then beats her. The queen happens to be driving by at that moment and hears the girl's cries, so she stops to find out what's going on. Ashamed to be caught showing anger to her lazy child, the mother says that she is beating the girl because she simply will not stop spinning; she claims that her daughter is, in fact, an excellent spinner.

The lie works so well that the queen commands the girl to come to the palace and spin there as she considers spinning to be a very salutary occupation. She's so keen on spinning as an activity, in fact, that she tells the girl that if she spins three rooms full of flax in three days, she may marry her eldest son (and, therefore, the heir to the throne).

Of course, the girl cannot spin at all. This is when the three spinners appear, three ugly old women who promise to spin all the flax if they can come to the wedding. They carry out their part of the bargain, and the girl keeps hers, inviting the women to her wedding. When the women appear, the prince asks them how it came about that one has a huge foot, another a huge lip, and the third a huge thumb. They point out that these deformities are the result of spinning the flax. The prince then forbids his bride ever to spin again because he wants her to keep her good looks.

What jumps out at us right away is that there is a difference between what men want from their wives and what women want from their daughters. The mother needs an industrious daughter; in fact, the queen thinks an industrious daughter-in-law is such a good idea that she ranks that virtue first. But the prince wants an attractive bride and cares nothing about flax. He is typical of a certain type of male attitude. The ugliness and deformity of the three "aunts" is, perhaps, a comment upon the way hard work can destroy women's good looks and even their health. But that seems to be the way the world works for poor people, and the ugly women don't complain: they just want to be invited to the wedding party.

In many ways this tale is a portrait of the different standards by which different classes live, which is presumably why the audiences who have heard it are able to smile and say that this is a reflection of the way the world works. Luck and good looks, and even a few well-placed falsehoods, plus a lot of hard work by some very under-appreciated people, have elevated many young women who were otherwise without particular talents to positions of wealth and influence. Supermodels, singers, and trophy wives are still around to remind us of that. Yet we cannot help but notice that the girl herself has not changed at all. She's still lazy. That is why I consider tales of this sort to be less useful, for all the sociological commentary they may carry with them.

So what is it exactly that makes "The Three Spinners" a lesser tale?

It has a plot in which the girl is sent out into the world, as an Orphan. She's set an impossible task. She gets supernatural help; she shows gratitude to the three spinners; and that leads to a happy ending. So far these are all standard forms of the tales. We can say, however, that the form is missing an important ingredient because the girl is completely passive and makes no effort to assert herself or her values in the tale. In fact, we can't even be sure she has values of any sort. There is no change or recognition in her. The magic solves the plot without revealing her character.

For that reason, it is worth stressing that the real power of the Grimm brothers' collection is contained within those tales that deal with transformation of character. That transformation is often signaled to the reader as an act of magic. Doubtless, in the past, some people must have thought that the young bewitched heroes and heroines were, literally, ensnared in magic. I would make the case, however, that the existence of spells in these tales is not to show helpless characters but to signify how changes can occur and how evil experiences have to be processed—in the same way that traumatic events in our time are seen to be worked out and exorcised in therapy.

Anyone with experience working with clients in a therapeutic setting will have noted that sometimes the changes a person goes through seem to happen, almost magically, in a very short amount of time, even though the work leading up to that moment may have taken years. It seems like magic, but it's the result of internal shifts and recognitions of a profound sort. These are not easy to explain or even to describe. In his song "Rock Steady" singer-songwriter Sting puts it this way:

> Woke up this morning and something had changed,
> Like the rooms in my house had all been rearranged.[1]

It's hard to describe change but easy to recognize it. The modern memoir and the trauma survivor's tale—typically, several hundred pages long—perhaps come closest to showing how this works in detail. And yet, how can one "explain" the action of a person who decides to go to Alcoholics Anonymous and give up drinking? How can one "explain" the way one person decides to give up narcotics while another cannot?

In some ways, of course, the comparison is not helpful, since the Grimm tales are concerned with growth rather than dealing with addictions. Yet, in each case, what matters is not so much the precise mechanics of the way a person can move to a better life but that the tales hold an acknowledgment that there is another, more productive way of being on the other side of the difficulty. When this happens it seems like magic.

This brings us to the story of "Rapunzel" (Tale No. 12). Most of us are familiar with the general outlines of the tale, but as in all such things, we need to be precise if we are to find reliable meaning in the narrative, so it's as well to go over the plot.

At the start of this story, a husband and wife long for a child, and eventually the woman becomes pregnant. One day, when she is looking out of her window, she sees some rampion (rapunzel) growing in the garden of the Enchantress next door and decides she must have some. Her dutiful husband clambers over the wall and gathers some for a salad. Obviously, this is a longed-for pregnancy, and he's eager to make sure the mother gets all she needs. The next day, the woman develops an even more urgent craving for the rampion, and, again, the husband obliges. This time, though, he is caught by the Enchantress, who orders him to hand over the child at birth.

In due course a girl is born and surrendered to the Enchantress, who names her Rapunzel. By the time she is twelve years old, the girl is already very beautiful. This is when the Enchantress places her in a tower without windows or stairs, and every morning comes to the base of the tower and asks her to let down her golden braids so she can climb up.

The king's son passes by one day, hears Rapunzel singing, and decides to investigate. He notes the way the Enchantress climbs up to visit the girl, awaits his opportunity, then follows suit. As soon as the prince lays eyes on Rapunzel he immediately wants to marry her, and she him, but they have no way of releasing Rapunzel from the tower.

Rapunzel instructs the prince to bring her a skein of silk each time he comes, so that she can make a ladder. Unfortunately, during a visit by the Enchantress one day, Rapunzel inadvertently blurts out that her captor is not as quick at climbing her braids as the king's son. Furious, the Enchantress cuts off Rapunzel's braids, moves her to "a desert," where the girl will later give birth to twins, then settles down to lie in wait for the king's son.

The king's son arrives in his usual way, climbing the braids that have been knotted around the window hook. He is confronted by the Enchantress and jumps from the tower, breaking his fall in a thorn bush. This bush saves his life but scratches out his eyes, rendering him blind. He then wanders, lost, for years until, by chance, he finds Rapunzel again, in her desert home. She is so moved she sheds two tears, each of which falls on his eyes, restoring his sight. They then marry and are very happy.

It's a tale familiar to many generations of readers. The theme seems to be that of longing. The birth parents long for a child, the mother longs for the rampion, the lovers long for each other. If we wish we can see this as a major part of the drama and observe that, when parents have invested a lot of emotional desire in an only child, they tend to be as over-protective as the Enchantress becomes.

For it is the Enchantress who places Rapunzel in her prison tower when she is twelve, around the beginning of puberty, and she's already beautiful, we are told. The Enchantress, as we already know, doesn't like to share anything, not even the plants in her garden. We can, therefore, see the Enchantress as an overly possessive individual. She represents the ways parents and parentlike figures can change when they're worried about their daughters' chastity. They become unreasonable and very protective and may insist too strongly on restrictions or curfews. Unfortunately, this is neither a foolproof method nor a good idea, as, later on, the convent-reared child is likely to be very easily led astray by others who are more sexually adventurous.

The king's son is certainly sexually adventurous. He has no hesitation in tricking his way to the top of the tower, then wastes no time in proposing—like the king who uses the password to gain entry to the house in the woods in "Brother and Sister," the tale that immediately precedes "Rapunzel" in the collection. The prince's furtive ascent of the tower is a direct mirroring of Rapunzel's birth father's clambering over the wall to steal the rampion in the first place. In each instance, the act is not exactly moral but it is a loving action.

Curiously, the king's son seems to delay before taking Rapunzel away. He could have returned the same evening with a ladder, but he doesn't, and some time later their love is uncovered. As we discover, they've already had sex often enough to conceive twins, so his delay may indicate something psychologically interesting, which is the way lovers, in their own private world of delight, lose touch with reality and do not do the "right" thing by society's standards.

This doesn't happen because the lovers are immoral. It happens because that's the way human beings act when they are caught up in their emotions. It's something we see everyday. Each year, thousands of young unmarried women in the United States become pregnant. This is not always because they're ignorant about birth control; sometimes, it's because their emotional state is such that they throw caution to the winds when in the grip of love. The figures suggest that this is not just a teenage phenomenon anymore. It seems to be what happens to lovers even in this day of contraceptives in every corner store.

I think it's important to stress this point because, in doing so, we can see that the love shared by this couple is a virtuous love, albeit naïve. The king's son may be an opportunist, but he's not a predator. They are both essentially archetypal Innocents and suffer years of separation before the story allows them to reunite. Rapunzel's tears restore the king's son's sight. Since he was clearly attracted by what he saw, it seems to be a fitting symbol for how attraction and infatuation can turn, at last, into real love, where the lovers see each other clearly for the first time. In his blindness, sight is replaced by insight.

More poignant, though, is the sense the tale conveys that any young lovers forced apart by severe parent figures may well be psychically damaged, living lives of longing for the lost love for years afterward. When seen that way, the king's son's blindness is emblematic of the inability of a thwarted lover to look on any other possible partner without thinking of his first love, with the resulting failure to move on with his life.

Both lovers, we notice, seem to be blighted by the Enchantress's veto of their union. Her major role in this tale is to stop people getting what they desire strongly, whether it be the rampion plant or Rapunzel herself, and she does this for no understandable reason. Who could possibly object to a king's son as a future son in law? Only a fiercely possessive parent who does not want her child to have any other attachments—ever. And only a vindictive parent would uphold that veto in the light of a daughter's pregnancy. With her private garden and prison tower, the Enchantress is someone who wants to possess and control things and people; she is the spirit of self-love that the young couple find themselves rebelling against. The tale, then, is about the real dangers to young people of overly strict parenting, and how young love, when cruelly thwarted, leaves scars on both the lovers—scars that can only be healed by bringing them together again.

I have worked with many people over the years, and all of them recall their first real love with extraordinary power. Almost all of them will admit that this first experience of love, even if it did not lead to a lasting relationship, shaped the rest of their lives in terms of the partner choices they made later in life. Some of them have subsequently spent decades looking for someone who is "just like" the lost lover. This is a topic that has garnered a huge amount of research. Elisabeth Young-Bruehl, for example, sees this yearning as a combination of chemically and hormonally based sensations and early imprinting.[2] It is very likely that the way we first fall in love becomes the pattern for how we will always fall in love, and broadly speaking that feels true for many people. It's a form of psychological conditioning. The number of people who carry romantic longings for former schoolyard sweethearts throughout their lives is, in some ways, touching. This is especially true if the attachment has not had a chance to work itself through but has been interrupted or cut short.

In a more sinister, negative context the same tends to be true of abused children, who have considerable difficulty overcoming their early sexual experiences and establishing healthy emotional ties later in life. They tend to repeat the pattern they experienced first. First love may have been romanticized by Hollywood, but we'd be wise to take the lesson that we are all, to some extent, shaped by our first loves and sexual experiences in ways we cannot always easily understand.

At its core, therefore, this tale tells us something important about love that our sexually free society tends to forget, and perhaps finds it more convenient to forget, as so many people seem to think they can erase their past and move on to the next partner. The story of "Rapunzel" reminds us of a basic truth of who we are, and it does so with a gracious lightness of touch.

Notice, the tale doesn't tell us what we should do. It doesn't say that there is a better way for parents to control their daughters if they are anxious about them, or that we can avoid the way a first love imprints itself on the brain. It tries only to portray the situation so we can be alert to what is happening.

A tale such as this would have clearly had significance for anyone who read or heard it at the time—parents routinely tried to control whom their children married, and still do today. This is not necessarily a bad thing, as any parent whose child has got in with "the wrong crowd" knows. The story seeks to show an extreme example of parenting in order to bring this tendency to light and make it available for discussion. In the process, it asks us to consider psychological aspects we may have forgotten to ask about.

Before we leave "Rapunzel," we have to deal with a technical objection to the form the story takes today, with the two lovers being separated, since this is a variant probably created by Madame de la Force, who published her version in 1698. According to Max Luthi, the Grimm brothers felt that theirs was, at heart, the true story rather than any of the other versions available and used it in that belief. Luthi argues that, in the other European versions, the lovers, in fact, escape using three tricks, which is "the clearer fairy tale structure, with its three beat rhythm."[3]

Luthi is right in pointing to the three-tricks escape as a familiar storytelling form, but that's no reason for it to be considered more or less appropriate for this tale. And even Luthi says of the Grimm brother's version, "But how captivating it is!" I'd like to use that as a reason to stay with this version. The tale obviously enchants and feels authentic in a vital way. The insights it sheds upon the way early love works are, it seems to me, worth having, no matter where exactly they came from.

It could be that the ending we have here came from another folktale, but we really have no convincing proof of that. For example, this ending is similar to the one in "The Girl Without Hands" (Tale No. 31), where the girl remains isolated with her child until the king finds her seven years later, and her hands grow back (although not because of tears).

In "The Girl Without Hands" there is an emphasis on eyesight, too, since the king finds his wife and does not recognize her. He then falls asleep with a handkerchief over his eyes. It falls and has to be replaced, and the girl tells her child to put the handkerchief over the sleeping king's eyes again. This happens twice, and the king awakens and recognizes the girl. With its emphasis on eyesight and seeing the loved one again, it's a remarkably similar ending in its general structure to that of "Rapunzel." We could, therefore, argue that this ending is also true to the spirit of older folktales, although Luthi conveniently ignores that.

This may make it seem as if I am selecting the facts to suit the situation; however, as we have seen already in this book, and will continue to see, elements in the plots of these tales tend to recur—in some cases, it feels as if endings have been lifted from one story and tacked onto the end of another. It's not always possible to ascertain what the "original" story might be. In any case, that isn't our main focus here. We're concerned with why, for two hundred years at least, these versions have been so full of meaning for so many people.

## CHAPTER 5

# Cinderella

## Sexual Maturation and Self-Empowerment: The Real Story

The story of "Cinderella" (Tale No. 21) is so well known that it has given rise to a whole school of thought, in which the "Cinderella syndrome" is viewed as the problem of young women and girls in our society who sit around, depressed, "waiting for their prince to come." The syndrome, however, has very little to do with the story, for, as we recall, Cinderella doesn't sit around and wait, she takes herself to the ball to encounter her future.[1]

This distortion of the famous fairy tale is nothing new. The story was well known even when the Grimm brothers were collecting their stories. It had been printed in a highly popular version by Perrault as early as 1697—nearly one hundred and twenty years earlier. Why, then, did the Grimm brothers include it in their collection?

Reading the tale, it immediately becomes obvious that there is a very solid reason, for their version is different in important respects from Perrault's. Perrault seems to have been the first writer to introduce the pumpkin, the fairy godmother, and the glass slipper into this ancient tale, and other details are changed, too. The Grimm brothers made a conscious decision to include a version of the tale they must have felt was more authentic than Perrault's made-to-please version. Whether it is, in fact, more "authentic" we can never truly know. We simply become aware that their version has real power where the other variant does not.

The following is a synopsis of the Grimm version; the scenario is the same as we recall. Cinderella is the neglected child of a man who marries again, and the step-mother and stepsisters are unkind to her, forcing her to sleep in the hearth ashes. The stepsisters are not ugly, however. The Grimms' version states that they were "beautiful and fair of face, but vile and black of heart." This is different already from the Disney version.

The father goes to the fair and asks the girls what they want him to bring back. The stepsisters ask for conventional items to please the ego—beautiful dresses and pearls and jewels. Cinderella, by contrast, asks for the first branch that knocks off his hat on the way home.

This is clearly a strange request, and we are certainly expected to question it. A man's hat is, to some extent, the symbol of his class and authority. This was definitely the case in nineteenth-century Germany as well as twentieth-century Europe in general. Only certain ranks of society were allowed to wear top hats, for example, while others had to make do with caps of various sorts, and the king's crown, of course, was the ultimate signifier of authority. The hat was a symbol of power, and when the branch knocks off the father's hat, threatening to remove his dignity, it indicates a challenge to the accepted order under which Cinderella lives.

The father returns with the gifts for the girls, and includes a hazel twig for Cinderella. She takes it and immediately plants it on her mother's grave, watering it with her tears, and it begins to grow. Her regular visits to her mother's grave, three times a day, signal to the reader that, whatever else Cinderella may be going through, she certainly can love and be loyal, and she knows that she is lovable, even though her mother is now dead and circumstances are against her.

As such, this is a reminder to us that the experience of being loved unconditionally by one's mother can be a powerful force that a child will internalize and use as a source of strength for the rest of his or her life, if need be. Cinderella never loses sight of this. The hazel tree grows, and in its branches appears a white bird that supplies Cinderella's wishes. This is the symbolic expression of this loving parental spirit.

When the ball is announced, Cinderella does not hang back. She wants to go and says so. The stepmother says she can only go if she can sort out the lentils that she just poured into the ashes. Cinderella calls to the pigeons and turtledoves to help her, and they sort out the lentils in record time. Pigeons are birds that mate and remain faithfully in pairs, and turtledoves have long been symbols of fidelity, since they mate for life. It's interesting, then, that Cinderella calls for help from representatives of the natural world that are also linked to loving fidelity and to the white bird that perches in the hazel tree.

The tale specifically tells us that "two white pigeons" arrive to sort out the lentils, then the turtledoves, followed by the other birds, so it is hard to miss this symbol. Cinderella is, of course, an example of fidelity herself—she regularly visits her mother's grave. The connection she has with the world of birds and nature tells us that, whatever else this tale may be about, it seems to be about the natural process of a girl's growth toward sexual maturity. For example, she knows she has to be at that ball. She doesn't know exactly why, but she feels this is her moment. The stepsisters, in contrast, are interested only in the chance to gain power and position if they happen to be chosen as the prince's wife. In Cinderella we sense a readiness and ripeness that will not be denied, even if she's not entirely sure what it means.

The stepmother is amazed that Cinderella has sorted out the lentils so quickly and sets her the task of picking another batch out of the ashes, twice as many this time, demanding that Cinderella sort them in half the time. She does so, once again with the help of the birds, who arrive in pairs, so we cannot help but notice the coupling symbolism again. Cinderella asks once more if she can go to the ball and is turned down flat. So she has made three determined requests, and these will be mirrored in the three days of the festival.

Cinderella has one more thing she can do. She goes to the hazel tree and asks for help. Notice she goes to her mother's grave and to the symbol of her mother's love (because the hazel tree is growing out of it), and the bird causes a gold and silver dress to fall into her hands, with slippers to match. And so she goes to the ball. No fairy godmother, no coach made of a pumpkin or rats transformed into coachmen. This is a different tale—one in which Cinderella takes a more active role.

The hazel tree is not a detail to be skipped over, either. Tale No. 210, the last in the collection, explains that the hazel is a sure protection against snakes, since in that tale the Virgin Mary was protected by a hazel bush. We have, therefore, another level of possible meaning, in which purity and protection from temptation are emphasized. This does not conflict with what we know about Cinderella—her purity and piety and the sense that her mother is somehow looking out for her.

Of course hazel trees have many other significances in many cultures, although one of the most prevalent is that water "diviners," or dowsers, who can detect underground sources of water, use hazel twigs held loosely in the hands. These twigs will twist, seemingly of their own accord, when the dowser walks over a water source. How this works exactly is something that science still puzzles over. It does work, however, and the water dowser would have been a familiar figure at any time during the past several centuries, whenever a well was required.

The hazel tree is a strong hint that the strength Cinderella draws to herself is the power of maternal love and also something as deep as the life-giving water itself, waiting in the depths for those who know how to tap into it. Cinderella is able to access the real strength of her deep, instinctual self. She knows it's time; and she knows what she has to do. This happens at a deep, unconscious level of the psyche.

At this point we have to recognize that the prince, also, seems to know it's time for him to marry. At a deep level, both these young people recognize their sexual maturity, and each is looking for a soulmate. This seems to be exactly what happens when they first meet, symbolized by the prince walking directly up to Cinderella at the ball, taking her by the hand, and refusing to dance with anyone else. The story is explicit about this. He doesn't change his mind. Instead, he declares, "This is my partner" on each occasion.

Cinderella certainly triumphs at the ball. On the first day, she leaves as evening falls, escaping the prince by darting into the pigeon house (often called a dovecote) and slipping out the other side. Pigeons and doves remind us again about the "pairing" motif. By the time the prince has had the dovecote broken open, she is long gone. Cinderella, we are told, takes her dress and places it on her mother's grave, from whence the bird takes it away again. The repetition helps us to cement the connection to the mother's love.

On the second day, Cinderella gets an even better dress, dances with the prince until evening, but at the last moment she gives him the slip outside the house. She shins up a pear tree, escaping back to her ash-covered hearth after having disposed of her dress the same way as before, and before anyone can see. The prince has the pear tree cut down to try and capture her, but she has slipped away while the workmen were getting their tools.

The actions the prince takes on both days show him to be more active than many other versions, and that's important. He doesn't just sit around and wait. He takes charge of his destiny, just as Cinderella does. Since both the tree and the dovecote are right next to the house, even Cinderella's father begins to wonder if it could be his neglected daughter who is causing the commotion with the prince. Perhaps in his core he recognizes something of her inner worth.

On the third day of the ball, Cinderella appears in a dress that is even more beautiful than before. When evening comes, she is anxious to leave and the prince lets her go. He's had the staircase smeared with pitch, so her left shoe, a golden slipper (not a glass one), is left behind. This is the final piece of evidence that allows him to turn up the next day at Cinderella's house and ask who owns the slipper.

Cinderella's three chosen means of escape are in keeping with the bird theme. In hiding in the dovecote, or up a tree, Cinderella is like a bird, and the pitch that glues her slipper to the stairs is symbolically like bird lime, which was used at the time to trap birds by sticking their feet to the branches they perched on. She is linked to the freedom and purity of birds yet again.

As we know, the eldest sister is the first to try on the slipper. It's too small, so her mother tells her to cut off her toes to make it fit—cosmetic surgery at its crudest, one might say. She rides off with the prince, but it's the two white pigeons perched in the hazel tree who sing out that he should look down to see the sister's bleeding feet. He does so, and he promptly returns her home. The same thing is repeated with the second sister, who cuts off part of her heel to fit into the slipper and is again detected by the pigeons.

Finally, the prince comes back and insists that there must be someone else in the house. A lesser man might well have given up at this point. But Cinderella eventually appears, clean and freshly washed, the slipper fits, and, we are told, "he recognized the beautiful maiden who had danced with him and cried: 'That is the true bride!'" He hadn't said this with the other sisters.

In fact, one wonders why the prince hadn't noticed the difference between the sisters. And here is the point. He had declared earlier: "No one shall be my bride but she whose foot this golden slipper fits," and having made such a statement he has to stick to it, even if it's flawed. He's a prince, after all, and he has to honor his word. When the wrong sister seems to be his intended bride he accepts it, although doubtless with some dismay. Remember: the sisters are beautiful but have "vile and wicked hearts" in this version, so the prince could, perhaps, be forgiven for at first agreeing. The Disney version has the sisters as such ugly creatures that we wind up thinking the prince is stupid as well as blind. It also distorts the theme that is so strong in this tale: outer appearances are not the only thing that matters. That is why his declaration that Cinderella is his true bride, and his recognition of her, is so important. He knows it's Cinderella he wants, even though she's far from well dressed, and he's absolutely certain that he wants her and no one else.

This in itself is a bold move for a prince—after all his bride must seem like a beggar, so how can he defend his choice? His courage never wavers, though. The prince has shown courage, and he's kept his word, even when he realizes his word was too rashly given—and that's an important lesson. In addition, he's also learned to distinguish between someone who looks good and someone who is good. He almost learned it the hard way.

Here we might consider the symbolism of the dance, which has for generations been a sign of harmony and of people being in tune, or "in step" with each other. As I'm sure we've all experienced, there are some people with whom we feel totally at ease when dancing, and there are others with whom it is torture. It reveals a possible correspondence between the physical and the spiritual realms. In the practical world, of course, this may not always be so, but we are in a mythic world, now, and so we have to see this as symbolic. What matters is not who we are or who our partner is; it's how we feel when we engage in the dance of intimacy with that person. It has nothing to do with rank, parentage, or money.

Another detail in this version of the tale is worth examining. Cinderella runs away when evening comes, rather than at midnight, which is what we see in the Disney version. Evening is a clearly defined time in a culture that has no easy access to clocks and watches. It's a normal part of the natural day visible to everyone. It also signifies the time when people go to bed, and nighttime and beds are all about where dreams and sex happen. Cinderella runs away just as it seems sexual contact of some sort will be likely to happen. Why is this?

From the point of view of the plot it's convenient. Cinderella's three visits to the ball allow the prince to show, three times, just how determined he is to be with her. Each of them is, therefore, an active participant in the search for the other. No passive sitting around exists in this story. This is, of course, the disadvantage of the fairy godmother versions of the tale—they make Cinderella passive and, therefore, we wonder why she would be worth loving at all.

It's surprising, then, that this bold young woman runs away when she could be making the most of the moment to secure her husband. If we choose to think mythically about the tale, we can see that there is a psychological truth that is being offered to us.

Cinderella may be ready to find her life-partner, but, as it is for anyone approaching marriage, there will be moments of panic when we feel like fleeing. If she just marches forward, then we have a tale that seems to give us a very bold but brainless young woman. Her flights, and her returns, tell us that she feels fear but that she overcomes it. She comes back to the ball twice after that first encounter; then, when the prince calls for her at her home, she doesn't run away and hide from him, she comes forward. The time is right. He's shown his love for her, and now she can reveal herself to him.

As any couple will tell you, it's a slightly frightening moment when one person wants to say, "I love you" to the other. Who will say it first? Should we wait for the other person to say it? Here, we have the same drama acted out in a different form. In his every action, the prince demonstrates that he wants Cinderella, despite her rags—there's the unconditional love she learned from her mother resurfacing in a positive form—and she now sees it's time to accept that this is what she deserves.

In the Disney version the ball takes place at night, which is all very romantic. Unfortunately, it obscures an important aspect of the tale, which is that Cinderella has to emerge from the half-light of the ashes and the fireplace and come into the light of day. She has to be "seen" fully, and that means allowing herself to be seen. She is recognized three times by the prince as the one he wants; then again, in daylight but in poorer clothing, she is seen again. The prince sees who she is, beyond the clothing. Daylight is emblematic of this. This is not about illusion and soft firelight.

At the wedding there is one further surprise, and it also has to do with seeing and daylight. The sisters decide to walk on either side of the bride, as a way of having everyone look at them. On the way to the wedding the two pigeons appear again, perch on the stepsisters' shoulders, and each pecks out one of their eyes. On the way back from the wedding, when the sisters are placed on the opposite sides of the bride, the pigeons appear once again and peck out the other eyes. The two people who had attempted to pervert the course of true love by tampering with the visual evidence, and for whom appearances are everything, are now punished by being deprived of their sight. This is fitting and also thematically useful. It is not the fine dresses or the physical beauty of Cinderella that win the day; it is that inner readiness and deep recognition that each partner has, one for the other.

Now, that may seem fine for a fairy tale, but can it tell us much about real life? Again, in working with clients, I can only say that, on many occasions, people have told me that they saw their future husband/wife and had a moment of inner knowing that seemed entirely contralogical, but which was too powerful to ignore.

One woman expressed it in this way. She was out on her first date with a man she wasn't sure she really felt was a good match. As they were about to cross a busy road to get to the restaurant, she instinctually reached out and grabbed his hand. She surprised herself, since she wasn't usually a "touchy-feely" kind of person, she said, and certainly not with relative strangers; but once they were hand in hand, she knew something had changed. And it had. They are, at this time of writing, very happily married and have been for a dozen years. I could give many examples, some of which are at first sight very odd, but the point would be simply that when the timing is right, and when deep recognition occurs, there is almost a duty to act upon it.

In terms of the six archetypes, Cinderella starts off as an Orphan in the truest sense of the word. Then she questions the existing power structure imposed by her stepmother, rebelling against it, in the same way a Pilgrim will question things, until she is ready to fight for what she wants. She grows her courage each time she goes back to the ball, so that when she is with the prince she is a Warrior united to the Lover aspect, a true Warrior-Lover. When she marries him she is, literally, going to be part of a Monarch pairing, and because she has seen the lowest depths of misery, as well as the richness of court life, she is, in many ways, the perfect queen.

For his part, the prince is an Orphan, "the King's son" who decides to reject the life set out for him and make his own choices in love. He follows his beliefs, not what is convenient, and he keeps his word, even when he makes mistakes. In searching for Cinderella he is a Pilgrim, seeking after his truth, and he demonstrates that he's willing to fight to win his bride. After all, he risks ridicule from everyone, including his father, for marrying a pauper. But he knows what he wants and needs. In his marriage he has demonstrated the qualities of the Warrior-Lover; when he becomes king, those same qualities will make him a superior Monarch. He can look beyond appearances and see the inner qualities of the person, and that is the sort of wisdom that is vital for any ruler.

The magic of the tale is that all nature seems to be in favor of this love match—the birds, the hazel tree, and the spirit of Cinderella's mother embodied in the tree. When we truly love another person, really there are no obstacles of any significance. And that's magical.

So let's spell it out: what saves Cinderella is that she is able to contact in herself, on a regular basis, that sense of unconditional love she received as an Innocent from her mother. She can return to that certainty, as she returns to her mother's grave, and it fuels her, sustains her, and provides the answers to her problems. For any of us, the strongest power we have is that confidence that comes from knowing that we are or were loved unconditionally. This allows us to love ourselves. Our task as we go through life is to stay in contact with this so that we can be guided by its power. Then the Magician archetype can break through.

Now, obviously, this version is qualitatively different from the Disney version or from the Perrault version. Those renditions are good in their own ways, but this variant seems to emphasize that the love Cinderella experiences is, above all else, a natural and normal attribute. The meaning of the tale seems to be that if we follow this deep feeling, if we trust it and honor it, then anyone who marries becomes a prince or a princess in terms of spiritual wellbeing and personal growth, no matter what their rank in life might be.

On the other hand, if you sit around and wait for your prince to come, or your fairy godmother to appear, then I promise you, you will wait your entire life in vain. We, each of us, have to reach into our souls and realize, like Cinderella, that we are worthy of love no matter what those who would wish to humiliate us might say. We deserve love, and we deserve to take action to go out and get it— but not in a random way. When we feel the time is right, then we have to take action. And that may demand courage. We may even have to go out several times before we find what we want. Moreover, when we do find the one we want and need, we may well be frightened, if only for a moment, that our lives will be taking a whole new direction. We may want to run back to our comfortable, familiar heap of ashes. But we won't be able to stay there.

To some extent, the story gives us a direct insight into the mind of the young person who becomes a Cinderella, sitting in the ashes, neglecting her appearance. In our terms, we might say that this is the child who dresses in all-black, who has skull ornaments and listens to music with dark overtones, and so on. This phase, whether we see it as gothic or depressed, is important because we could say the individual is engaged in a type of mourning, a little like Cinderella is for her mother, as a protest against a world that does not see her or recognize her feelings. We have to bear in mind that not only do her stepmother and stepsisters ignore and mistreat her—so consumed are they in their pursuit of what is conventionally prized—but her own father doesn't see who she is, either.

By retreating to live among the ashes, in her own world, Cinderella is protesting the unacceptable values she sees around her. How is this different from the lonely child who prefers video games to people? It seems surprisingly close. It seems even closer to the recent Japanese cult of the "Emo," young people who dress in gothic styles and who place more emphasis on their own emotions (hence "emo") than on their social responsibilities. There have been violent scenes when "ordinary" citizens have decided to chastise and beat these young men and women.[2]

Yet Cinderella herself is loving and seems to have no trouble being loved by the birds who help her. Does that make her an anomaly? Hardly. I live close to Harvard Square in Cambridge, Massachusetts, and I can see quantities of young folks, alienated, confused, tattooed, and with multiple piercings, any day of the week, clustered in one of several meeting points. These are perhaps rebels who have yet to find a cause. Speaking with them, I'm sometimes surprised at how gentle and kind they are behind the façade. The story of Cinderella suggests that what these young people are missing is love and self-acceptance to help them heal their sense of woundedness, to help them out of the ashes.

Whenever I'm teaching this story, or talking about it to groups, a specific objection often bubbles up. People tend to complain that Cinderella finds her prince too easily and that the immediate succumbing to love at first sight is delightful but not likely to happen to most of us any day soon. This is a valid objection. It could equally apply to any of the stories where the main characters seem to fall for each other within seconds, and that's most of them.

This objection only has substance if we are dealing with the real world. The first person you meet at a dance, who happens to be powerfully attracted to you, may not be the best possible spouse choice. Everyone knows this, and most assuredly everyone living in the Grimm brothers' time knew it, too. We could choose, instead, to view the love-at-first-sight theme in the Cinderella story as symbolic of something rather different—the sense of knowing that can hit us at certain times, which we feel we must follow.

Central to this story is a truth that lies at the heart of all storytelling: we all know things that we don't even know we know, at least not yet. The story reminds us of the wisdom we have that we perhaps choose to rationalize away and ignore. After all, if we are being logical, then Cinderella should give up in her attempt to go to the ball since she has neither clothes nor shoes. But she doesn't let that get in her way, and these things are provided for her. Her confidence in who she is and what she must do, and the prince's answering certainty, tell us that some things defy easy explanation.

When the time comes, we'll know; after that, we'll just have to take a leap of faith.

This leaves us with one loose end. Cinderella is often linked to birds, and we need to ask why. Even her running away at dusk seems to be a version of the birds going home to roost at evening. Birds are, as we've seen, symbols of freedom. They are also images of the soul. Jesus, when baptized by John, received the Holy Spirit in the form of a dove, and so the dove subsequently became an image on almost every church baptismal font; it would have been a very familiar echo for the audience to pick up. In this tale it is suggestive of Cinderella's mother's spirit. In addition, birds have very obvious breeding seasons, which coincides with the theme of readiness. We could, therefore, see the birds as representing the spirit of nature, of God, that guides us when we are attuned to our own natural rhythms. Seen this way, the birds that peck out the stepsister's eyes do so because the sisters have offended against the right order of the world, hacking at their feet and denying love in their selfishness.

This is a powerful love story, one that can reach deep into the psyche and which is alive for us today—if we are willing to take a closer look. Again, it's not about princes rescuing paupers. It's about trusting our own internal sense of self, so that we can become a prince or princess in the running of our own relationship. That depends, as we've seen, on recognizing unconditional love. We've all experienced it, but most of us have forgotten what it feels like.

## CHAPTER 6

# "The Girl Without Hands"
# and
# "The Robber Bridegroom"

## The Question of Good and Evil

By now it should be clear that one of the greatest achievements of the tales we've been examining is that they can deal with the larger topics of life in an extremely succinct form. In addition, the tales are frequently filled with violent and disturbing scenes. For example, in the story of "Hänsel and Gretel" (Tale No. 15), the children are led into the woods by their father and stepmother because there is not enough food at home, and so they are going to be abandoned there to starve or be eaten by animals. If this tells us anything it would be that life was extremely hard for the poor and that, in such a world, children were sometimes seen as expendable. The basic ferocity of some aspects of human nature is acknowledged as being just below the surface.

If we can see the world of Hänsel and Gretel as predatory, then we can also note that the tales have no hesitation in dealing with the topics of Good and Evil. In the strange story of "The Girl Without Hands" (Tale No. 31), which we mentioned briefly in Chapter Four, the Devil claims the girl after tricking her father, but the girl is so good and forgiving that the Devil can't carry her away, and she even allows her father to cut off her hands so that the Devil cannot claim him instead. She then wanders the world and meets a king who marries her and gives her silver hands. All does not continue well, though, because the Devil forges letters when the king is on a trip and orders her killed. She escapes because the king's mother has pity on her. She then spends seven years in exile, attended by an angel. Eventually her hands grow back, the king finds her, and all is well.

It's a peculiar tale—one in which we notice that the girl herself is almost completely defenseless (as symbolized by her lack of hands), even though she is attended by an angel all the time she is away from human beings. It is as if the tale is saying that innocence and goodness are at the mercy of anyone who wants to do them harm. We could, therefore, make the connection that people who help the girl are performing the task of angels, and that angels only appear when there's no one else to do the job. It is an interesting way of thinking about what charity means in terms of human society; namely, we have a job to do in helping our less fortunate fellows, and it's a holy duty.

Goodness, therefore, is seen as fragile, even helpless. Goodness, in the form of this girl, cannot even look after itself very well, and since she needs help she brings out the goodness in others. It's elegant. The seven years it takes to find her again after the Devil has meddled with the letters lets us know that, once evil has crept into even the most blameless of lives, it takes a long time to clear it away, and that goodness must be actively sought out. This is a true statement of the way things seem to be. A good name can be tarnished in no time and take years to be reestablished.

We can also notice that the son the girl bears is named "Sorrowful" for a reason. We can see him as being born into a world that already has evil in it, so even though he himself is not evil, he suffers from it, too. Even if we are not guilty of anything, the effect of evil is to create sorrow around us. Yet the miracle in the story is that the girl grows her hands back. This is not just a convenient reward for the girl. It may, in fact, be telling us that the normal condition of the world is that good people are routinely the victims, but that when we see how things are and accept the sadness of an imperfect world, we then become stronger. Heartache can hurt us, but it will make us stronger and less helpless, and we can regrow our faculties to cope with it.

Now, this is a complex idea expressed in a short tale. It deftly describes the problem that goodness faces in the world—a quality that seems so vulnerable and helpless.

This leads us to the question: how does one deal with evil? The great power of these tales is that they never for a moment doubt that evil exists, and that it is brutal and savage. In this attitude the tales are different from some of our more recent sociological theorists, who have tried to suggest that evil does not, in fact, exist. To them it is simply the effect of a society that is not properly regulated.

There are several tales that approach this question: the famous story of "Bluebeard," who kills his wives (the Grimm brothers did not include this story); the Grimm fairy tale entitled "Fitcher's Bird" (Tale No. 46), which is a variant of "Bluebeard"; and the tale we will deal with next, "The Robber Bridegroom" (Tale No. 40), which is a third variation of the story of "Bluebeard."

In "The Robber Bridegroom," a young woman is to be married to a man who seems like a good match as far as her father is concerned, but she feels some doubts about him. One day the prospective groom asks her to come to his house to meet his guests, saying he will strew ashes on the path so she can find her way. She is uneasy and when she reaches the edge of the forest she has a pocketful of peas and lentils that she drops to mark the route.

When she arrives at the house it is empty except for a caged bird that sings out that this is a murderer's house. In the cellar she finds a very old woman who confirms that this really is a murderer's house and that she has had to cook for him for many years. As they speak the robbers come back with a beautiful girl they have captured, and the old woman hides the would-be bride behind a large barrel. The robbers then proceed to strip their screaming captive, and in a scene that seems to be a version of a rape, they give her enough wine to kill her, then they cut her up and begin salting the flesh. The salt reference is interesting because, according to ancient legend and superstition, the Devil cannot stand salt (hence the habit of throwing spilled salt over one's shoulder into the Devil's face). So we're being told obliquely that these cannibal robbers are not devils but humans.

At this point one of the robbers sees the dead girl's ring, uses an ax to try and cut off her finger, and the severed finger flies through the air, over the barrel, and into the young woman's cleavage—"the bride's bosom," as we are told. The robber is about to go searching for it but the old woman calls him to supper, telling him to wait for morning and the light. Fortunately, the old woman has put a sleeping draft in the wine, so the robbers all doze off, and the two women escape. By now the ashes that marked the path have blown away, but luckily the lentils and peas are still there and have even sprouted and grown up, we are told, so the two reach the village again safely in the morning.

The girl tells her father everything, and they hatch a plan. The wedding celebration goes ahead, but the guests are all asked to tell a story. When her turn comes, the bride says she has only a dream to relate, then tells the tale of her night in the murderer's house. When she gets to the part about the finger flying through the air and into her cleavage, she pulls out the finger itself, complete with the ring. The guests jump up and seize the murderer, and he and his whole gang are executed.

Obviously, this is a tale about predatory and savage people—about real evil—and it asks us what we are to do about such things. To understand the story fully, we must once again look at it from a mythical point of view.

The first thing that must strike us is that the girl has misgivings right from the start. She may be inexperienced, but she's not naïve. Like Hänsel and Gretel, she makes sure that she marks a path so she can return if need be. There's an interesting contrast between the deathlike associations of the ashes strewn through the forest and the peas and lentils she takes with her, which have started to grow by the time she returns, and so are definitely representatives of life. This is a tale that centers on goodness and life outwitting evil and death.

The young woman's actions show that she may be an Orphan, but she's not stupid. In fact, her ability to question and doubt makes her more of a Pilgrim, especially as she makes her way through the dark forest. It must have taken courage to do that. When she reaches the desolate house, the caged bird tells her to flee from the murderer, but she doesn't. After all, a bird can be taught to say anything, so it may not be reliable. Yet if we think about this symbolically, we could also see the bird as a representative of the natural world who has been imprisoned in a cage and forced to speak out about the unnatural horrors that have been happening in the house.

The young woman continues to search the house and finds the old woman in the cellar, in the deep dark recesses of the house. The old woman has presumably not been eaten or sexually assaulted because she's too old and unappealing, but she feels she can't leave. Now that the young woman has arrived, the old woman knows she has a place she can flee to and a route to follow to get there, which is why she is eager to help the young woman.

We might say that the old woman represents what can happen to the weaker partner in an abusive marriage or domestic situation. She doesn't feel she can leave, she can't stand up against the evil things the man does, and she becomes ancient and helpless before her time. Perhaps she represents the young woman's potential destiny.

If we accept this, we could say that the murders that have been happening in the house are symbolic of the type of victimization of women endured in any marriage that kills their spirit, leaving them as helpless Orphans in their own homes. In our age of battered and brutalized women, some of whom are battered to death by their domestic partners, it doesn't take much imagination to link the ideas we have before us here to our times.

We should notice, also, that this scene of rape, murder, and cannibalism takes place in the basement of the house. These are the dark lawless recesses of the human soul. What can we possibly learn from them? To some extent, the sexual urge felt by those who are about to marry is lawless and fierce. The desire to possess the other sexually, to revel in the pleasures of the flesh, is a feeling that marriage seeks to regulate and to confine. The young woman comes face to face with the darkest aspects of what should be a life-giving and affirming feeling that can build trust and love. As a woman who will marry someone one day, she is being given an important lesson in the ways desire can be debased into mere lust and destructiveness.

It's a lesson we must all face since we must all learn the difference between sex as an exercise in power and domination, and sex as a loving act. The young woman has seen the darkness that exists in the soul of each of us, and so is unlikely to make a mistake in her own life, later. She has met her shadow self and has not given in to it.

Meeting the shadow, and not giving in to its lawless appeal, is the task of the

Warrior-Lover archetype, who must choose what is right and fight for it. Our young bride has achieved that, for, whenever we reject an option that is evil or debased, we are not just saying "no" to what is wrong but saying "yes" to what is right.

The detail of the severed finger falling into the young woman's bosom is hardly accidental, either. The finger has a ring on it, which makes one think of wedding rings, but it also lands near the woman's heart, the organ that symbolizes love and trust. The butchered girl might well be another deceived fiancée. As such, this detail serves to let us know that the woman is wiser and more cautious—just—than other girls, and that she is going to carry the lesson she learns close to her heart, forever.

Many stories might end with the escape of the young woman and the old woman, perhaps with each carrying a sack of looted gold; not this one. The wedding goes ahead but, in this case, only in order to capture and punish the wicked. This is, to some extent, pure practicality. We need to make our charges of wrongdoing in public and supply proof (in this case, the finger) in order to redress evil. At a time when men and women were sometimes simply declared to be witches and were punished without any evidence, this is a surprisingly sensible way forward.

The larger point is made in the process. Evil exists, yet it cannot be handled successfully by the individual acting alone—it has to be exposed with the help of the whole community. This way the young woman can be reassured that it was not her fault for getting into a difficult situation. If the whole community gets together and identifies the wrongdoer, there is far less possibility of self-blame. This is an important point as, in situations of spousal abuse and rape, the victim can frequently wind up feeling she is somehow responsible for what has occurred.

In my work with clients who have been sexually abused, the victim often has the sense that she is to blame, that she (and it is a female, usually) must have provoked the attack, and that she is "damaged goods," as a result. This is most likely to happen when the attack is kept secret or not spoken about publicly. What we have in this story is an example of how to deal with that possibility.

Once again, it's the severed finger that makes the difference. The father cannot pretend it doesn't exist and cannot pretend that the old woman is a figment of the imagination, either. By making the accusation public in this way, the young woman sees the reaction of the whole community and is supported by it. It also effectively deals with any feelings of self-recrimination the young woman might have that she brought this event upon herself by not trusting her own intuitions enough at the start. Remember: the caged bird the young woman meets first at the house tells her the truth—but she does not believe it! She is, therefore, an example of how accusations, no matter how true, can be disregarded, and she herself might have suffered from people disbelieving her, but for that finger.

If we wish to see the tale in terms of the archetypes, once more we could say that the young woman refuses to be a passive Orphan, accepting without question the man designated to be her husband. Her intuition tells her all is not well, so she takes along the lentils and peas, just as a safety measure. She navigates through the dark wood, explores the cottage, and shows herself as courageous and questioning—indeed, a Pilgrim who wants to discover the truth.

Fortunately, her courage gives heart to the old woman who is, one might say, without hope—an Orphan who can find nowhere else to go. It is the old woman's idea to hide her, to distract the robbers, and to slip them a sleeping draft. Courage can breed more courage. When the pair flee, they walk all night and arrive at dawn at the village, so we can see that daylight and goodness are overtly linked, and that the pair are moving toward goodness once again.

The young woman wastes no time in telling her tale, and whether she organizes the sham wedding herself, or her father does, it is she who uses the subterfuge of the dream to make her accusation face to face. Again, this takes considerable courage. We could say that the young woman is asserting values that are worth defending and, by extension, are necessary in a real marriage based on mutual affection—values that are absent in the robber's house.

She is a Warrior-Lover at this point. When she makes her case, she mobilizes her entire community to make a moral decision, thereby allowing her to move into the Monarch archetype. She doesn't need to pass judgment; the robber is judged by a jury of his peers. The situation itself calls for its own remedy. This is not a crude tale of revenge but of the reestablishment of right actions in a functioning society; that, in itself, is a kind of Magic.

The tale can be seen as a simple cautionary tale, but I think we can also see that it explores the nature of evil and how to confront it successfully. It also examines the problem of the damage that can be done to those who are victimized by spousal abuse and rape, and how to make sure the wrongdoers are punished while the innocent are left unscarred by the act of reporting the wrongdoing. This is an issue still being debated today, of course, when allegations of abuse in our legal system often leave the person who has been wronged feeling even more damaged than before.

It would be easy to discount this tale by simply saying that the ending is a basic act of revenge upon the guilty person, and that this is a familiar ending, used in both "Bluebeard" and another tale: "Fitcher's Bird." Certainly the endings to both tales are very similar. Yet, in each case, the story ends by having the community or family asserting that murderous behaviors are not acceptable. In "Fitcher's Bird" the wizard's entire bridal party is locked in the castle by the relatives of the bride, and then the castle is set alight, killing the wizard and all those who must have been quietly complicit in his repeated marriages to newly abducted young women. In "Bluebeard," the bride's relatives arrive when summoned and kill Bluebeard, thereby saving the woman just as she's about to be killed. This is not revenge; it is justice.

This leaves us with one more detail to consider. The young woman feels that something is not right with her groom, but she goes to his house, anyway. She reaches the house, and the bird tells her to leave; however, she doesn't. At this level the story tells us that if we trust our instincts, they will help us to avoid trouble. This is what we ought to do, but we don't. That's the way we so often are: we discount our gut feelings. It is part of the tale's wisdom that it acknowledges this fundamental human failing.

Certainly it's more prevalent than we may think. In an informal survey I've made of all the divorced people I've known well enough to ask, I've questioned them about their first, failed, marriage and whether they had any doubts before the wedding. Every one of those questioned said words to the effect of, "I knew this wasn't a good idea even on the way to the ceremony." One woman found herself in the car heading to the church, hoping that some sort of disaster would put the ceremony off—she envisioned an attack by terrorist fighter jets. Now, this sort of thinking may be hindsight, or it might just be that so very often social pressures cause us to override our better instincts. After all, in the tale, the young woman's father thinks the groom will be a good match; that can be persuasive.

The clear hint is: listen to your intuition and avoid evil when you can. And yet, we have to say that if the young woman had run away at this point there would have been no possibility of growth or self-empowerment. Just as the divorcees in my survey learned some important spiritual and emotional lessons from their failed marriages, so too the young woman can only learn if she goes to the place of difficulty and despair. The safe route in this case is actually the route that offers the lesser opportunity for growth. If the young woman leaves, she'll simply go back to her father, as a good Orphan, until he finds her another dubious suitor. Ghastly as the tale is, it lets us know that we all have to face extremes, things that could destroy us, so we can grow, make sense of what happened, and heal.

The two tales in this chapter are fascinating because they represent two very different ways of dealing with the problem of evil. In each case, the evil comes from a father's mistake. The girl without hands is promised to the Devil as the first creature that greets her father, and the Robber Bridegroom is the father's choice of husband. In each tale, the girl is innocent of any wrongdoing; yet, there the resemblance ends. God and angels reward the girl without hands, while it's the girl's own efforts that solve the problem of the Robber Bridegroom. These seem to be completely contradictory messages—one type of advice for the spiritual realm and another for the practical world.

If we take this idea a little farther, what we see is that in both tales the concern is that the injured person does not get further injured by the process of putting things right. Put another way: the girl without hands does not allow her situation to turn her bitter; instead, it makes her more saintlike, and although she feels sorrow, her psyche is not blighted. In contrast, the brave would-be bride in "The Robber Bridegroom" pursues a course of action that reduces any possibility of feeling guilt and diminishes the amount of self-loathing she could bring to the situation. The message seems clear: do not stoop to revenge; there are better ways—ways that are less costly to the psyche.

One tale is spiritual advice about dealing with the general tendency of the world to create evil, and how one can face it. The other is worldly advice about a specific instance of evil. The tales do not, therefore, contradict each other; instead, they make a valuable distinction, suggesting the qualities we can mobilize in ourselves to overcome very different problems.

CHAPTER 7

# "Little Snow-White" and "Allerleirauh"

## Sexual Rivalry, Narcissism, and Incest

Following on from the themes of good and evil in "The Girl Without Hands" and the murders and cannibalism of "The Robber Bridegroom," we recognize that the Grimm brothers' tales deal with some very murky human passions. For example, the famous story of "Little Snow-White" (Tale No. 53) views the sexual rivalry between a stepmother and her daughter as murderous. Certainly, if we care to look, we may see mothers and stepmothers who are envious of their children just about everywhere; however, very few stepparents actually murder their stepchildren. It's clear, then, that the extreme actions described in this tale serve to highlight the situation for the reader. Extreme or not, these passions are worth looking at more closely.

The tale is familiar, but we may want to be clear as to what exactly the Grimm brothers recorded. In their version, a queen sits by a window, sewing. She pricks her finger and three drops of blood fall in the snow. She wishes for a child "as white as snow, as red as blood, and as black as the wood of this window frame." The daughter who is born to her has white skin, red cheeks, and hair as black as ebony. Unfortunately, the queen dies and the king remarries. The new queen is beautiful but "proud and haughty," and we are told that she "could not bear that anyone else should surpass her beauty." Her magic looking glass tells her she is the fairest of all, until Snow-white is seven years old, at which time the mirror tells the queen that Snow-white is now more beautiful.

Enraged, the queen calls a huntsman and asks him to take Snow-white into the forest and kill her, and to bring back her lungs and liver for her to eat. Clearly, this is not just ordinary dislike but pathological hatred. It suggests the wicked queen feels the child to be a threat to her very existence. Fortunately, the huntsman lets Snow-white go and takes back a boar's lungs and liver instead. This is when Snow-white wanders in the forest until she finds the cottage of the seven dwarfs, and they make

83

her their housekeeper. The magic mirror, though, reports that Snow-white is alive still, and so the wicked queen goes to find her.

She next appears before Snow-white disguised as a peddlar selling stay laces, which she ties around Snow-white so tightly that she collapses as if dead. The dwarfs return and loosen the stays, saving the girl's life. When the mirror tells the queen she has been unsuccessful in her attempt, and that Snow-white is still the fairest in the land, she returns with a poisoned comb. Snow-white places it in her hair and faints away—and again the dwarfs return just in time to save her.

As before, the queen gets the news from her mirror, and this time returns with an apple, half of which is poisoned, half of which is not. Disguised again, she offers Snow-white half, while eating the other part herself to show it is safe. Snow-white eats the apple and falls to the ground, lifeless, and it seems the stepmother has succeeded.

This time, the dwarfs cannot revive Snow-white. In their grief, they can't bear to bury her in the ground and, instead, place her in a glass coffin on a hillside. That's where the king's son finds her, asks the dwarfs for the coffin, and prepares to move it. The jarring dislodges the fragment of apple in her throat, and Snow-white awakes. The pair marry, and the wicked queen comes to the wedding, full of fear and rage, where she is punished with red hot shoes that cause her to dance herself to death.

It is interesting that, in "Little Snow-White," the stepmother has a magic mirror that she consults, which tells her she is the fairest in the land until she's eclipsed by her stepdaughter. This constant mirror-gazing is an indication of a major force that runs her life: narcissism. So what does that mean?

We can say that the narcissistic mother is so self-involved she is never able to become a supportive parent in the real world. In her narcissism, she cannot see her daughter as separate and independent; instead, she always treats the child as an extension of her self-worth and, therefore, of her self-love. If the daughter then leaves and has her own life, the mother will likely become violently angry, and even though the competition is no longer evident to anyone else, the mother will still see it as vital to destroy or control the child.

This is what we see in "Little Snow-White"; it is certainly what we observe in our present-day world, with its numbers of mothers who see their children as only having worth if they reflect well on the mother—who retains a position of superiority. Whether the mother is overprotective or controling, the effect is essentially the same: the child is kept down, dependent, and inferior. It may not be actual murder, but its effect can be to destroy the soul of the child.

Obviously, this is strong, disturbing material. Many people who love their mothers may find this unacceptable as a starting point, which is why the tale changes the mother into a stepmother. It's easier to accept this kind of behavior when the person is not one's blood relative but simply playing the role of parent. It's also more "realistic," since there is sometimes considerable friction between stepparents and stepchildren. We do not have to go too far in our world of divorced parents and blended families to see as many instances of conflict as there are of harmony.

In our present-day world, we can see this in the mother/stepmother who feels that her children have to be "a credit" to her and do as she wishes, no matter what the child wishes. This is the mother who schedules far too many activities for the child because this is what is socially expected of the family in their demographic. It's all about *her*, not about what the child might want.

A common version of this is the mother who wants to be the daughter's "best friend" and support her in such things as sporting endeavors. Such a mother will organize teams, travel thousands of miles, and sacrifice countless hours of unpaid time to shepherd and promote the child's career. She does this because she is the mother of the star player, and everyone had better pay attention to that! In this way, she gains social status that puts her daughter in the shade to some extent. The mother seems to be doing everything for the child but, in fact, in some instances, she is controling the child, who has to buy into this "game" and who does not have the option of failing or opting out. Give up? After all I've done for you? Not continue, after all we've been through? We can imagine the dialogue. These are things we see around us everyday, but they are not the less damaging for all that.

In the tale a more suggestive layer of meaning can be seen when the stepmother disguises herself three times as a peddler of various objects aimed at killing Snow-white. The first thing she sells the child is a set of laces for a corset, or stays. Children were often made to wear dresses that had laces or fastenings at the back of the bodice, as a sort of looser, junior version of the tighter adult clothing. Some of these laces could be brightly colored. The stepmother fastens these new laces so tightly that Snow-white falls down in a faint and is in danger of dying. Fortunately, the seven dwarfs appear and release her.

This can be seen as the temptation of adult, and sexualizing, clothing. Stays have only one purpose, and that is to distort the body by squeezing in the waist and pushing up the breasts, and the tighter they are laced the more they accomplish this. But this is hardly age appropriate. Snow-white is still referred to as a child in the story, and she has been a threat to her mother since the age of seven, so even at this stage she cannot be old enough for corsets and push-up bras. She is repeatedly referred to as "little"—we must remember that the full title of the story is "Little Snow-White"—so we're left in no doubt as to her youth and relative immaturity. Of course, she's interested in what grown women wear: what little girl hasn't played dress-up with her mother's clothes? But here the innocent game has taken a more sinister turn.

One can't help thinking of those children who today are entered into beauty pageants, made up and sexualized before their time, and the damage that can do to the psyche. And this is often done simply so that the parents can look good, for their own sense of pride. The stay laces are therefore a metaphor that signals the way a child can be "shaped," or forced into being something she is not yet ready to be; they are also a metaphor for how that shaping, if done too early, can kill the spirit of any child. Children, of course, are often only too willing to conform to what adults want, and that is part of the tragedy. They will give away their individuality in order to please their parents.

This happens because of the under-developed ego of the child. Unfortunately in our own time the child's compliance is often used as an excuse for the parents' own behavior. Parents will claim the child loves hunting (said of a nine-year old girl who had just shot her first wild boar, reported in *The Boston Globe*), or that the child truly loves a certain sport, when what is actually happening is that child is seeking to please the parent and be close to him or her. It's a tricky balance, and the tale is sensitive to this in a way that is surprisingly sophisticated.[1]

The second attempt to kill Snow-white is made with a poisoned comb, which the dwarfs see and remove just in time. Again, the assault is all about physical good looks—utterly consistent with the way the narcissistic queen thinks. As we know, girls aged nine and up are often absorbed in the way their hair looks. The queen is, in fact, symbolically introducing Snow-white to her own realm of obsessive physical grooming—the realm that helped turn her into the monster she is.

Once more, the queen both wants Snow-white to conform and to kill her, and, again, we see the metaphor of destroying the spirit. Hair, as any parent knows, can be a challenge, since combing it is a way of "taming" its wildness—a description that can be applied to the hair of many children. The stepmother is once more attempting to take the child into a realm of control, where she can be tamed. We might say, therefore, that by having the girl conform to this way of thinking, the queen would indeed be killing the free-spirited creature that is Snow-white. Interestingly, the dwarfs again save Snow-white. It's almost as if the childlike, living-in-the-forest eccentricity that puts them outside the realm of normal human relationships is the only thing that can save her. They help Snow-white to reject these poisoned "adult" gifts.

At this point I'm reminded of my own schoolyard experience, where we all ran around as slightly wild kids of nine or ten, and where having one's hair combed was as much a trial for girls as for boys. Then, one day, one of the girls turned up at school with a full perm. She kept saying that her mother didn't want her to join in our scrappy games because they would mess up her new hairstyle. Her resolve lasted until about lunchtime. The next day, she appeared and said that this time she really couldn't join in the games because her mother had been annoyed at her yesterday. Once again, her determination wore thin and, by the end of the day, she was racing around with the rest of us. The third day, she appeared wearing a new sweater that she had promised her mother she wouldn't get dirty. This time she didn't play with us at all. With each succeeding day she looked a little sadder, standing to one side, looking on. Well, we were kids, and we soon forgot to include her in the way we had before. Not even the whole schoolyard of playful dwarfs could bring her back to being the authentic kid we had taken for granted all that time. She was no longer herself; she was her mother's creation.

The last temptation is, of course, the apple, half of which is poisoned. Apples given by tempters can only make us think of Eve in the Garden of Eden being tempted by the serpent. In this case, like Eve, Snow-white is unable to resist. It's hard to avoid seeing this as a metaphor for sexual temptation: the half of the apple that the stepmother consumes, which is not poisoned, symbolizes the experience of sex when one is older and ready for it; in sharp contrast, the part of the apple that Snow-white eats, which is poisoned and sticks in her throat, indicates to us that, at this age, she's simply not ready for sex yet.

How can we understand this? In the modern world there are certainly those self-absorbed parents who would be only too happy to see their child behaving in a sexually superior way, as if she knew more than other girls her age. This gives the mother the chance to seem superior, too, and to dominate the child, who now has to depend on the mother for advice since none of her peers can be much use yet.

In fact, it's another route to crushing the child, another form of murder of the spirit. Certainly, we can see this whenever youngsters go through that ritual of American high school life, the junior and senior prom. The girls are dressed up in adult and often provocative styles; they often look rather nervous about this and try hard to cover it up. From my own observations, and from talking with friends who are parents, as well as with school teachers, questions frequently arise around the ritual of the prom concerning how some of these young people will cope with the sudden expectations of being "adult" and sexual. Some are ready, while others may be chronologically old enough but not emotionally equipped yet. Rushing a child toward sexual activity often leads only to lasting confusions and loss of self-worth. This can be as destructive a force as anything a young person can encounter.

In the story the dwarfs return, find Snow-white seemingly dead, and are very sad. They place her in a glass coffin, where she can still be seen. Notice that the dwarfs are male, but they are hardly full-grown representatives of the male world; they are, in some ways, neutered males. Today, we may find a version of this among women who prefer to spend their time with gay male friends, or with men who are not perceived as sexual but as eccentrics or clowns. Snow-white is still a child, but her stepmother's dangerous need to be admired for her beauty—by men, we must assume—has caused Snow-white to settle for companions who can admire her for her housekeeping and not respond to her as a person who will one day grow to be a sexual individual. She's found a nice, safe place to be, even though the temptations of the world of sex are beginning to make themselves felt as appealing. After all, she *likes* the stays and the combs.

Similarly, the children of narcissistic parents will, sometimes, at a certain point, deliberately choose to stay "young" in demeanor and lifestyle. In this way, they avoid claiming their true selfhood as young men and women, since that would offer a challenge to the attention that is focused on the mother. Here, though, we have to be careful because the dwarfs in the tale of "Little Snow-White" suggest something more. They clearly love her, so we might say that they are safe males who offer her unconditional love and acceptance. In this way, they can be seen as exactly what Snow-white needs in order to recover her mental well-being after the assaults of her stepmother. Just like the girl in the schoolyard all those years ago, what Snow-white needs in the early part of the tale is to be a happy child accepted by her peers. That, in part, is what lies behind the symbolism of the dwarfs arriving and saving her twice. They offer her the love she needs at that stage in her life.

It's only when a real man, the prince, appears and the coffin is moved that the apple is dislodged and Snow-white comes to life again. "Dislodged" is probably a euphemism for vomiting the apple out. Psychologically, Snow-white has reached the point where she can reject the unhealthy aspects of premature sexualization that have sent her into a form of shock. She's been in suspended animation—one way to describe the period of latency that typically occurs between about the ages of about 5 and the onset of puberty. She's not been inert; she's just been maturing quietly without much visible outward sign.

Another way of considering this is to say that fear and early sexual trauma can sometimes delay the onset of sexual maturity in young women. The start of menstruation may be delayed, perhaps for years. Sometimes fear shows itself in other ways, too. For example, a young woman who has been frightened in this way may present herself as highly made-up and attractive-looking but behave in a very cold and rejecting fashion. In this case the young woman is not able to be fully present to life. Her behavior signals that she can be looked at but not touched—the glass coffin in which Snow-white lies is an effective symbol of this mental state.

Now that she's ready, she meets her mate. The safety and love provided by the dwarfs have permitted her to break free of her stepmother and grow to such an extent she can be ready to love. Her girlish self has "died," and she has spent some time taking stock of herself—symbolized by her time in the glass coffin—and the woman is now ready to emerge from a period of latent growth.

This story is about many things, yet one of the most prominent of the themes is how young women can be damaged by the self-involvement of those parents whose actions can harm their spirits. Fortunately, in assessing the problem, the tale also tells us what the solution is: safe and unconditional love.

When I worked with disturbed adolescents, there were several young women who seemed to be in this situation. One, in particular, had been recruited by her mother as a prostitute, around the age of twelve—she had been given the sexy clothes, the provocative haircut, and told how to act. The girl had been terrified by this; yet, at first, she had gone along with the mother's wishes. Of course, she had; after all, this was her mother and, at that age, this is what one does. It must have taken considerable courage, but she managed to run away several times and was eventually taken into care by the authorities.

At one point, before she ran away, she placed padding under her clothing so that she would look like she was pregnant, in the hope that this would cause men to leave her alone. In an action such as this we are reminded of the glass coffin, which signals that anyone can look but they may not touch. What the girl needed in order to heal was to feel safe, and to know that men were not going to try and push her into bed at every opportunity. She seemed to need the unconditional love she hadn't got from her same-sex parent, and she seemed to need the space to be a child.

If these examples seem extreme—and the tale itself is one that has extreme actions in it—we may want to try and tie the story closer to everyday life. Not everyone has a narcissistic parent, after all. And yet every parent has the tendency toward narcissism—a tendency that needs to be fought. Parents derive a certain amount of status from having a child. If that child is attractive and amusing, then the mother, in particular, will be seen as fortunate. The mother, of course, will want the child to grow up and do things the way Mother thinks best. This is basic socialization and also a shaping of the child to what's best for the mother, so inevitably the desire to control and mold is always present. The problem is getting the balance right between socializing a child and coercing him or her.

The stronger the mother's will, or the deeper the mother's need, the harder it will be to achieve this balance. By shifting the actions of the tale to the stepmother, it becomes easier to consider the ways in which every parental relationship contains a germ of narcissism, waiting to grow if given half a chance. If we see this as only an issue pertaining to stepparents, which it often can be, then we miss the fact that it arises in almost all parenting situations. In fact, it is a perfectly normal part of the psychology of parenting, and one that has to be addressed if the child is to be emotionally healthy.

And that brings us, inevitably, to the question of Snow-white's father. Where is he in all this? He's remarkable because of his absence. He should be protecting his daughter, but he's nowhere to be seen. The stepmother managed to snag him in marriage, presumably because she is beautiful, and her sense of being valued would come, in part, from his placing value on her. If she were to be valued for herself by a loving partner, rather than having to ask the mirror for confirmation of her worth, we would have a figure who does not need compulsive reassurance. The stepmother needs acceptance and unconditional love, just as Snow-white does; instead, the adult takes her frustrations out on the little child.

In our own times, there are numerous examples of celebrities sacrificing their children's well-being in order to increase their own high profile. Stars, from Britney Spears to Tom Cruise and Katie Holmes, have used their children as a way to gather more photo opportunities. Britney Spears, a fragile woman who seemed to have no sense of what a child needs, actually lost custody of her children because her own life was in such emotional turmoil. She wasn't short of money or opportunity; she simply didn't know who she was when the cameras weren't on her.

The children of celebrities never really escape their famous parents in our culture, and sometimes their desire to shape themselves in the image of their parents can cause them to have stunted lives. How exactly does anyone follow a charismatic and attractive parent who is a leader? Following the assassination of President John F. Kennedy, the rest of the Kennedys have sometimes tried very hard to be successes, but some of them don't seem to have been personally happy. The second George Bush was not the leader his father was; Julian Lennon is not the musician his father was, and so on. One wonders what will happen with Chelsea Clinton, daughter of two very high-profile figures. It's not that these children can't be successful and happy; it's that the accident of celebrity birth makes heavy demands on them.

Those demands, to some extent, exist in any family. As I write this, in late 2009, the tabloid press informs me that actress and singer Cher's daughter, Chastity, who at one time came out as a lesbian, has begun the process of undergoing sexual reassignment surgery and becoming a male named Chas living in a heterosexual partnership with his girlfriend.[2] Since Cher is notable for her cosmetic surgeries, including the removal of ribs, and for various enhancements that make her look far younger than she is, we have an interesting situation. We could see her daughter's actions as a desire to follow her mother into cosmetic surgery, as a wish to steal her attention, and, in this final form, also as a rejection of some of her mother's values of what "'looking good" means. I doubt that we'll ever know the exact details. All we need to observe here is that a parent who is overly involved in her own appearance and success can be a difficult parent to grow up with and leave the child with a real identity problem.

Before we leave "Little Snow-White," we must take a look at the ending of the story. There, we discover that the queen is so enraged that Snow-white is alive, she can hardly bring herself to go to the wedding. When she does, "she stood still with rage and fear." But a judgment awaits her: red-hot iron shoes are fastened on her feet, and she is forced to dance until she drops down dead.

It's a ghastly parody of the wedding dance most normal mothers would enjoy, as they cede pride of place to their daughters. As a metaphor for the way narcissistic people will work ever harder at making themselves the center of attention, even when that attention is grotesque, this scene is eerily appropriate. Narcissism is seen for what it is—sterile and self-defeating. In some ways, the story is about how, very often, narcissists are terrified by their own bodily aging and the prospect of death, and how sexual jealousy becomes their chosen way of expressing this fear.

The Grimm brothers did not stop at these considerations, though. In the rarely told tale of "Allerleirauh" (Tale No. 65), they raise the topic of a different type of sexual tension: instead of a mother's narcissism, we have a father's incestuous desires.

The German title of the tale translates as "all kinds of fur," an allusion to the fur cloak the girl wears. It's a strong tale, similar in form to "Cinderella," in which a king promises his dying wife, who is beautiful, that he will never marry anyone less beautiful and with less wonderful golden hair than hers. No one can match these standards until the daughter grows up; the king notices that she is more beautiful than her mother and has the same golden hair, so he decides to marry her.

The premise of the story is that the king has promised his wife to obey her dying wish but also is required as sovereign of the realm to have a wife. At first sight, it seems as if he's caught up in his duty to two imperatives that exist outside himself; yet, as we see, he is the one who decides that the new bride has to be his daughter, against all protestations from his councilors and against the moral commandments contained in Holy Writ.

The daughter buys time by ordering three splendid dresses and a cloak made of sections of fur from each of a thousand species of animals living in the kingdom. This fur cloak links the daughter to the natural variety of the entire animal world, as if to say that the incestuous wishes of the king go against everything in the whole of nature. Once she has her clothes, she puts them into a nut shell, then she takes a golden ring, a golden spinning wheel, and a golden reel, and leaves.

She finds work in a nearby castle after huntsmen in the service of the neighboring king find her asleep, wrapped in her cloak, and think at first she's a wild animal. She works in the kitchens, covered in ashes and soot, until there is a grand ball (plenty of echoes of "Cinderella," here). Begging for half an hour to go and see the occasion, she dresses in her first beautiful dress, washes her face, and dances with the king, who is enchanted. She then runs away to her "den" (the animal references are repeated), and changes back to her dirty clothes.

While the cook takes time to go and see the ball, she gets to prepare the king's soup, and she places her gold ring in the bottom. The king loves the soup even more than usual and calls for the girl. She appears, looking filthy—she's called "the hairy animal" by the cook—and denies any knowledge of the ring. The next time there is a ball the same thing happens, except with the second dress. The king is enchanted and again the girl runs away after half an hour and changes to return to the kitchens.

Once again a kitchen maid, this time the girl puts her golden spinning wheel in the soup. Again she is summoned and denies everything, and again everyone thinks of her as "the hairy animal" because of her cloak. A little later, there is another ball, and the girl uses her third, most beautiful, dress. The king greets her, holds her hands tightly, and slips a ring on her finger when she isn't looking. But she escapes and has only time to fling her fur cloak over her dress before she has to make the soup again. This time, she puts her golden reel into the bowl. Again the cook calls her "fur-skin" and "witch." The king finds his soup to be even more excellent than before, sends for her again, and this time he notices the ring as well as a finger she forgot to make black with dirt. He sees the star dress she has on underneath her cloak and recognizes her as the girl with whom he has danced. They marry and live happily ever after.

It's a tale that is, in some ways, so similar to "Cinderella" that one could be forgiven for not paying attention to the details; yet, it is from the details that some important things emerge.

The father's incestuous urge is depicted in powerful terms. Even though everyone is revolted by the idea, he is determined to go ahead, and he even has excuses to back him up. His choice of his daughter has some logic to it, but it's a logic that is estranged from reality and morality. In this, he is a frighteningly accurate rendition of the way a man's sexual urges can adopt what looks like reason in order to get what he wants. This is the thinking of the incestuous father who argues that he can't get what he wants from the mother, so he is entitled to get sex from the child. In the cases of incest I've dealt with this seems to be the predominant rationalization. The tale is eerily accurate.

The girl does the only thing she can do: she leaves. She takes the dresses because she knows, somewhere deep down, that one day she'll need to reclaim herself as an attractive woman; but, for now, she's so frightened she can only show herself as a rather unpleasant animal in her cloak of all the different furs.

In terms of the psychological effect of attempted incest, this rings true. Young women who see that they are valued only for their physical beauty can, on occasion, elect to disguise this, either by dressing badly (as the girl in the story does), or by putting on a lot of extra weight, or by behaving in ways that are unappealing. The woman who uses her extra girth as a way of making sure she isn't attractive to men is a commonplace of our times, and certainly we've all seen young people who have chosen to dress in ways that seem to challenge any socially accepted standards of what is attractive. When a trauma such as incest has occurred women very often don't want to be considered attractive because they fear the attention of men. I once worked briefly with an adolescent girl who was very beautiful but whose behavior was such that she was thoroughly nasty to all men. The message was clear to every male: go away because you're all perverts.

The early exposure to incestuous tendencies can take many forms, of course, but the tale doesn't attempt to define them all—simply to show one strong example, so that we can make the connection.

The tale three times mentions bowls of soup, and we have to ask what these could mean. As we've seen, the young woman turns out to be better at making the soup than the cook. This could signify many things, one of which is that she is learning, while in the kitchens, about being a nurturing and caring person. The objects she places in the soup are, therefore, pretty heavy hints that she wants to be discovered, and that she wants to be appreciated for being more than just a good cook or a pretty face. She just doesn't know how to say this any other way.

This is exactly how it is with those suffering from trauma. They want to be helped out of their misery, and they give hints that they are ready to be helped, but they are afraid to act on those internal promptings. The young woman's actions are a way of asking for help without actually asking for help.

So that leads us to look more closely at how she does this. First, she uses the ring in the soup, something precious hidden in something humble. It's a good description of her own disguise. In addition, any ring is always a potent symbol, linked as it is to marriage; and the spinning wheel (how one gets that into a bowl of soup I'm not sure) suggests the work of unmarried women, spinsters. The golden reel of thread may also be seen, if we choose, as the thread that runs through everything, or perhaps as the product of successful spinning. This is the private code or poetry of signs. She use this specific vocabulary to say that she wishes to be recognized and "seen" fully, and the vocabulary a person chooses in these circumstances will tend to be as specific as the person. For our purposes, we can say that these are all objects that are domestic and have to do with productive labor. Finding a rusty nail in our soup invites a different message than finding a golden reel.

PRINCES, FROGS & UGLY SISTERS

How can we understand this better? I recall working with a young woman, many years ago, who used to dress in what looked like black rags. For a while, she was fiercely critical of me, but I was encouraged by this because it signified that she had at least noticed that I existed; she could have ignored me. Her dismissive attitude offered a starting place for a dialogue; this was her "poetic" way of telling me she might one day want to trust me. By being critical, for instance, she wanted to see if I would get offended and reject her. This was her pattern: she'd push to see if others would accept her, no matter what. It was a way of looking for the unconditional love she hadn't got as a child. I learned later that when she had arrived at this particular group home, she had refused to wash for weeks, until the other girls dragged her into the showers and scrubbed her. This might have been frightening at the time, but she said to me later that "it was the best thing that ever happened to me; they showed me they cared."

This has to remind us of the young woman in the tale, who, when asked by the king who she is, says: "I am good for nothing but to have boots thrown at my head." She repeats this three times. Obviously she doesn't really believe it, but like the girl who had to be dragged to the showers, she wants someone to react and show real caring.

Over time, the girl I worked with in the group home began to criticize me less. Our encounters became more interesting, and we talked about many things, including cars. Then, one day, she brought me the hood emblem she'd stolen off a car that matched my car. Here was a gift that was also stolen property, and it was clearly a test to see how I'd act. Would I reject it? Would I report her? I did neither. I chose to overlook the small crime and see the gift as a gesture about our friendship that she didn't know how else to express. It was "secret" because I didn't report her; yet, it was not about the ornament but about the privacy of her trust. I give this example because it shows how those who have been mistreated and sexually frightened try to communicate a tentative sense of trust and connection. It matches the girl in the tale rather well.

When this girl left the group home, it was clear we had built considerable amounts of trust, to the extent that she felt better about herself and about men generally. She still had some problems; for instance, she beat up another member of staff fairly thoroughly after she felt she'd been misunderstood. The key word here is "misunderstood." Like the princess in the tale *understanding* was all she wanted, but she didn't quite know how to ask for it. This is why the king for whom she works has to act cautiously. He has to show that he understands her skittishness; when he slips the ring on her finger, he's giving her a gift, too, even though she can't see it right away.

The tale might almost be seen as a handbook on what one needs to do in order to rebuild the shattered sense of trust that comes with incest or sexual exploitation. It takes time, it means appreciating the gifts the other offers in an indirect fashion, and it eventually takes firmness.

The king certainly shows this. At the climax of the tale, he tears off the fur mantle of the princess's disguise and reveals her in her real glory before everyone, in her "star-dress" with her golden hair. The woman can no longer use a disguise to hide from herself. It's an elegant metaphor. To some extent, we all want someone to help us become our true self, to be seen as we are; and many of us are afraid to ask for that help.

To consider this tale in terms of the archetypes within it, we have only to see the young woman as an actual Orphan, temporarily housed as a kitchen maid, to appreciate her courage in seeking out the king. She is a Pilgrim, and this is her pilgrimage. Seeking him out three times, she alerts him to what is going on, and he comes half way, one might say, to meet her. Each is asking to be seen, but each is also about to take a Warrior-Lover's risk, one that may involve disgrace and rejection.

The king suspects that the kitchen maid is the beautiful woman with whom he danced, and takes a risk following through on his suspicions. He's not fainthearted, and neither is she; yet, their actions demand courage—the girl could be scorned and the king's reputation and prestige undermined. Instead, they have the courage to act upon what they know to be true. Together, they become Warrior-Lovers, ready to make the transition into Monarchs. After all, she's a princess and he's a king, and they are ready now to take up their proper roles in the world. In seeing her quality, the king is able to demonstrate his ability to trust his own excellent judgments about others and their worth regardless of what they look like—the Monarch's task *par excellence*; and in overcoming her own fear of the tyranny of her father the king, his mad fixation and extremism, the princess demonstrates that she has grown personally, too, and is not just judging by rank. Archetypally, these two are equals.

This tale has been largely ignored over the years, and I think that has to do with the incest theme, which most people would rather not address. It functions, however, as a sort of partner pair to "Little Snow-White", which deals with a self-involved and destructive female parent, while "Allerleirauh" deals with an exactly equivalent male parent. The beauty of these tales, and the courage of the Grimm brothers in selecting them, lies in the fact that such important issues are not swept under the carpet. If we wish to understand a father's overinvolvement with a favorite child, and what the result is likely to be, and if we want to know how to put that right, then "Allerleirauh" is an important tale.

## CHAPTER 8

# "Hans the Hedgehog" and "The Donkey"

## Parental Rejection and the Recovering of Personal Authenticity

"Hans the Hedgehog" (Tale No. 108) has a strong appeal because it is so odd. Its challenging nature leads us back to it even though, in some ways, it is not an attractive tale.

Hans is born as a result of his parents' wish to have a child, even if it turns out to be a hedgehog, which is what his father rashly says one day. Now, European hedgehogs are actually rather gentle creatures, frequently friendly to humans, and in no sense predatory. The nearest they come to that, according to country lore, is in being able to lick the teats of cows when they are lying down in order to get a drink of milk. But they are very spiky and, when afraid, will roll themselves up into a defensive ball of spines. They are not at all like porcupines, which are known for formidably defending themselves. European hedgehogs can be picked up using bare hands, even when rolled into a defensive ball, as long as one is gentle. This might be a clue we can use later in assessing this tale.

Although the parents are horrified at Hans's appearance, they decide to keep him, for he's human from the waist down and hedgehog from there upward. Hans is baptized (which shows that his parents regard him as human), but he's obviously not exactly what they want. At a certain point, Hans asks for and receives a set of bagpipes. He then asks for the cock to be shod with iron shoes, like a horse, and for some pigs and asses, and says he'll head off to the forest with them. He sits astride the cock and goes off into the dark forest, where he ends up sitting in a tree, playing his bagpipes, while his livestock multiplies beyond all expectations. His parents are relieved he's gone.

Up to this point, this is obviously a peculiar tale, until we reflect that the bagpipes make Hans a close cousin of the god Pan, a Greek nature and fertility god who played his panpipes made of reeds in the forest. This explains Hans sitting astride the cock, an obvious symbol of sexual power. In Roman and Greek depictions Pan and his satyrs appear as half-man and half-goat. They are renowned for their sexual energy and so are often shown with huge erect penises. The way Hans's flocks of pigs and asses multiply seem to link him firmly to this myth.

After a while, a lost king appears and asks Hans for the way out of the forest. Hans agrees to supply directions if the king will give him the first creature that greets him on his return home. The king agrees but writes a bond in which he inserts the all-important word "not." Since the king's daughter is the first creature to greet him on his return, the king is happy with his sly action, and the daughter agrees that this was well done.

A second king then appears in the forest, and he, too, asks for directions. Again, Hans shows him the way out and makes the same conditions. When this king reaches home his daughter is the first to come out and greet him. He tells her of his promise, and she agrees that such a promise must be kept, even though she doesn't like the idea.

At this point, Hans decides to return home for a visit. He takes his vast herd of pigs with him and gives them to the village to kill. He has his cock reshod with iron shoes, and travels on. His father is once again relieved he's gone, and he offers no expression of thanks for all the pork his son has supplied.

From here, Hans goes to the castle of the first king, where he's met with armed soldiers with pikes—an echo of his own spiny situation. Seated astride the cock, he flies over the soldiers into the castle and demands the king give him his reward or he says he'll kill both the king and his daughter. The first king is terrified and tells his daughter she must go with Hans to save his life. So she leaves in a coach with Hans, his bagpipes, and his cock.

Then, we are told, "a short distance from the town, Hans the hedgehog took her pretty clothes off and pierced her with his hedgehog spikes until she bled all over. 'That is the reward of your falseness,' said he, 'go your way. I will not have you!'" This is the scene that probably repels most readers. It's a humiliation that is also a sexual assault, especially when we read that the daughter is "disgraced for the rest of her life." It's also a key scene, and we'll return to it.

Hans then travels to the castle belonging to the second king. Here, in contrast to the first castle, he is greeted with joy by the king and his daughter, and the daughter agrees to marry him, even though she is terrified of him. He instructs her not to be afraid—before he gets into bed with her, he will creep out of his hedgehog skin, and four men should be ready to take it and throw it on the fire.

Everything takes place as Hans describes, and he takes on human form, except for the fact that he's coal-black. The physician arrives next morning and puts salves on him. Hans gradually becomes white and, we are told, "a handsome young man." The daughter is delighted, and the marriage is now "properly solemnized." Several years later, Hans and his bride visit his father, who at first does not recognize him. Eventually, he is convinced that this is his son, and they are all happy.

In some ways, this tale is very similar to another one that appears later in the collection, called "The Donkey" (Tale No. 144). In that tale, a king's son is born as a donkey, learns to play a lute, and when he wins another king's daughter—the king offers her to him—he sheds his donkey skin and becomes human. In that tale the king himself steals the skin and burns it, the donkey having shown a desire to return to his hairier identity during daylight hours.

These are both transformation tales. They have a lot in common with "The Frog-King," although "Hans the Hedgehog" certainly has more violent undercurrents. The skin-shedding motif is also found in the tale of "The Goose Girl at the Well" (Tale No. 179), in which the beautiful princess puts on the skin of an ugly goose girl after she has been rejected by her father. It's remarkably similar to what happens in the tale of "Allerleirauh," in which the princess wears a cloak of fur, as we have just noticed, as a form of protection.

If we are to find meaning in all this, we might want to think in terms of the sexual references that are so plentiful. The Pan-like Hans, with his pipes and his gift for making creatures breed, is a symbol of both the energy of sex and the socially unacceptable part of it, its animal insistence. As we recall, both kings in this tale want to find their way out of the forest. In a difficult circumstance we often have to get help from some very unlikely people, and we can't ignore them later because it's not convenient.

Similarly, we occasionally have to trust our instincts, especially when we are confused, and if we trust those feelings to show us the way "home" then we cannot pretend later that they are not an essential part of ourselves, and that they do not have a claim on us. The kings in each case could have ignored Hans, but they don't—they take his advice. Hans, remember, is a normal male from the waist down. He just isn't civilized; he's a wild man. But he can become civilized by being accepted, treated with respect, and loved, which is what the second king and his daughter offer. Seen this way the story of Hans can perhaps emerge as symbolic of how we all have to integrate the wild and untamed part of ourselves into the psyche, so that its energy can fuel our lives and allow us to find our 'home'—our personal sense of authenticity.

Under these circumstances, the daughter's sexual anxiety is all too understandable; it's also an anxiety that many young women feel when they think about men and sex for the first time. The task, perhaps, is to look past the fear of sex and to see something else. The princess may not love Hans yet, but her loyalty to her father is a loving act. The "good" daughter is, therefore, able to help transform this rough diamond into something far more acceptable because she is prepared to suspend her judgments about him.

How can we understand this? Just consider: there are plenty of young men out there in the world today who wear disguises that are every bit as frightening as Hans's spines—spiked hair, wrist bands with metal studs, Mohawk haircuts; we have seen them all, and they go in and out of fashion. The behaviors of these young men and women may be unpleasant, the tattoos and body piercings excessive, and some may even look downright frightening; yet, in each case, this is a reflection of feeling unaccepted at some point in their very early lives, just as Hans was. We'll recall that because of his spines, Hans's mother could not even suckle him at her breast. That is the most basic and primal form of acceptance, and failing to receive it is a great loss to the individual in terms of being able to feel love and express it.

This brings us back to our somewhat frightening youngsters of today. The message many of these young people send is: "I will repel you before you have a chance to reject me, and that puts me in a place of greater power." It's a logical form of self-protection. It should come as no surprise, then, that Hans is so infuriated by the first king and his daughter. They have regarded him as inhuman, merely based on his appearance. This is a sensitive subject for him, for he is still human, he has saved the king's life, and he deserves respect. Many people who behave in ways that are designed to outrage others are, in fact, simply asking to be treated better than they have been—they just don't know how to ask for that directly. To some extent their defenses tell us about the depths of their longing.

The second king's daughter is both honorable (she upholds her father's promise) and loving. She keeps the promise because she loves her father—"For the love of her father, she would willingly go with Hans if he came," we are told. She knows what love is, and it isn't the shallow self-interest of the other king and his daughter. It is this love that allows Hans to put aside his outer skin—his layer of psychological defenses—and become fully human; it gives him back the other half of himself. Notice, though, that the shed skin has to be taken away by four men and burned. It suggests that the defenses we have, even when willingly laid aside, have to be completely removed or we may want to creep back into them. If four men take them away, then Hans won't be able to leap up and fight them off, and the fire will consume the defensive outer layer he no longer needs.

This is the central psychological insight that is mirrored in the much shorter tale "The Donkey," where the bridegroom each morning sneaks back into his donkey skin. What this strange detail conveys to us is that, often, when we shed behaviors that we have adopted to preserve our wounded sense of self, we can feel very naked. Hans, for example, remains in bed, even after he's lost his hedgehog skin, suggesting that he's not yet completely healed. The physician comes and gives him lotions and salves until he turns from black to white. This is a way of saying that we can give up certain behaviors, but we will still have vestigial amounts of them until we allow ourselves to be healed.

An example of this might be the man who has a beard as a way of avoiding being seen fully by others. He can shave off the beard, but that does not necessarily mean he can be more open with people, so that his soul can be seen. That might take more time. The beard's removal is the first and perhaps most symbolic step, but it's not the whole change, not yet. In the tale we're told that the physician washes Hans—a sort of second baptism that removes the past, making him free.

In a culture such as ours, where men—and, sometimes, women—dress in ways that are as much disguise as anything else, this tale conveys some useful truths. In any town in the United States or Europe, we can see men and women wearing the shirts of their favorite sports teams, complete with the names of their favorite players on the back. This is a way of dressing up in order to take on the power of that player, by association. What we see is the coded version of who this person would like to be, rather than who this person actually is. As such, it functions in the same way as Hans's hedgehog skin: to show one aspect of the person while concealing others. Taking on a persona is both necessary and, to many people, confusing. We can all become so attached to our public self that we forget what our private self might be.

Several recent television shows have become popular by building on this idea. They all seem to be focused on the "makeover," whether it be of the person's wardrobe, makeup, hairstyle, or home. Particular examples are *Extreme Makeover* and *What Not to Wear*, as well as such shows as *The Biggest Loser*, where contestants compete to lose the most weight for prizes.[1] Closely allied to these shows are those that tell us how to beautify our homes for successful sales. In all these programs, people are shown by experts how to dress better, be sexier, live in neater homes, and so on. And at the end of each program, we see that transformation and are impressed. What the shows don't tell us (at least not very often) is what those people are like a year or two years later. Have they been able to maintain their new version of themselves? In some cases, I'm sure they have crept back into their hedgehog skins.

One program on the US channel BBC America, *How Clean is Your House?* has the formidable British female hosts giving direction as to how to tidy up houses that are every bit as scary and revolting as Hans's skin.[2] In almost every case, the home clutter and disgraceful housekeeping are a symptom of an underlying problem in the relationships of the people who live there. A half-hour television show can't always solve issues of squalor that stem from damaged self-esteem, after all. The tale of "Hans the Hedgehog" acknowledges this. He needs more than just one dramatic action to break free of his old "self." He needs the healing salve, too.

Behind this lies a more benign truth. The tendency of little boys to be scruffy and dirty and rather unpleasant is well known. "Slugs and snails and puppy dog's tails, that's what little boys are made of" goes the nursery rhyme. Add to that the way little boys are interested in their genitals, tend to like phallic objects such as sticks and toy swords and enjoy waving them around, and we begin to see that the sexuality of little boys can be rather obvious and perhaps off-putting.

But that's just the way things are. In adolescent males, the stare, the wolf whistle, and the crass pickup lines may function to show sexual interest is present, but they are often so blatant as to succeed only in repelling the opposite sex. Not many girls respond positively to such attentions. The tale of "Hans the Hedgehog" suggests that we sometimes have to accept this rather blatant sexuality, seen here in Hans's unattractive exterior, and have confidence that it will be able to be transformed by love into something more acceptable but just as vital.

This brings us back to that troubling scene in which Hans spikes the first king's daughter and disgraces her. We could view this as humiliation, a misogynistic piece of revenge, and leave it at that—that would certainly be in keeping with the somewhat fierce tenor of this tale; yet, I think there is more here. We notice that the deceitful daughter is not even prepared to be open to the possibility that this strange-looking creature is worthy of anything remotely resembling positive regard; in fact, she rejects him even before she's seen him. Compare that to the second daughter, who agrees to marry Hans despite being trembling and fearful. She even tells Hans that she is afraid, but she does not set her mind against him. Is that weakness? Or is it courage? Eventually, of course, her love does succeed—he sheds his defenses and shows his softer aspects.

Perhaps the hint we need is this: if we want to know the transformative power of love, then we have to remain open and risk being hurt. If we can't be vulnerable, then we can't be real. We risk hurt, but without that risk what can possibly happen that is genuine? The first daughter has set her mind against Hans completely, so he rubs her nose in her prejudices. That's painful because, when we come face to face with our own lack of generosity of spirit, it is always humbling.

The second daughter moves forward in a more open way, and her rewards are far greater. Hans, after all, seems to know he can be transformed. He's the one who gives instructions about what is to be done with his spiny skin. He knows what to do, he's ready to do it, and all he needs is someone to be open enough to help him do this, so that he can be vulnerable. He's had plenty of experience of others rejecting and lying to him, even after he has done good deeds, so this is a leap of faith, but he seems more than willing to do it.

Those who have exiled themselves from society's idea of normalcy need to be coaxed back into a productive relationship with the rest of the world. We all know that. To some extent, we've all lived this if we've insisted on being ourselves. We cannot buy our way into the good opinion of others. We see this in the tale when Hans offers his gift of swine to the villagers and is rewarded only with his father's relief that he is leaving again. Most of us have felt something like Hans feels because most of us have differentiated ourselves from the mainstream at some point and consequently felt like "outsiders," especially as we were growing up. Giving people gifts in the hope that they'll like us is very often a complete waste of time and effort: it incurs a sense of obligation in the receiver, and it allows the giver to hide behind the gift. It's when we ask others to see us as people, no matter what we look like, that change can happen and acceptance begin.

An example may help here. A man I knew who was somewhat shy used to try very hard to be helpful to others. If anyone needed something done in terms of fixing a car or digging the garden or needing a ride somewhere, he was there. He hoped that his actions would cause others to love him. The trouble was that they merely felt obligated toward him. He was generous, certainly, but because he was always giving, he didn't allow anyone to see who he truly was, and he never asked for help with anything himself, even when he needed it. Everyone thought well of him, yet almost no one wanted him around.

Things started to change only when he found he had to ask for help with certain things when a relative fell ill. At first, he was mortified to have to ask at all, but when he did, he discovered that people were, it seemed, relieved to be able to give something back. For the first time, they had begun to see him as a person, just like themselves, and that opened the door to acceptance. Hans the Hedgehog, with his twice-repeated statement to his father that he was leaving and they "would never see him again" is like that. It's equivalent to saying, I don't want anything from you again. But he does. He comes back to see his father (with the gift of the swine), and then he comes back again later when he is married. That little detail in the story is vital. He does want love and acceptance, even though he claims the contrary.

Those times when we are at our most prickly and rejecting are when we are at our most needy. A best-selling novel by Muriel Barbery makes this same point. *The Elegance of the Hedgehog* is the tale of two people who are in hiding from a world they see as idiotic and unsympathetic.[3] The title refers to their mannerisms, which they wear as a disguise; yet, each is waiting for a chance to move out of this hidden life, and each is very like us, the readers. The metaphor still has relevance.

Viewed this way, the Grimm brothers' tale is a well-considered depiction of the defensiveness found in those who feel they have been rejected, and it is a tale that also suggests very directly what can be done to save the situation. What readers do with these insights is up to them; however, I think it's evident that the tale is an invitation to look beyond obvious human behaviors into the motivations and needs behind them. Once again, the story has a sophistication that is more than we might have expected from German peasants living in a limited world of hard work and shortages. But that's our prejudice. There is no reason to believe that their poverty and distance in time should make them less perceptive that we are.[4]

As an archetype, Hans is an Orphan right from the start. He goes into the forest as a Pilgrim, and while he's there, playing his panpipes, he seems to come to know who he is. After all, he's not lost, as the kings are. He can find his way back to civilization at any time; he just isn't sure he can manage it just yet. So he tries offering the gift of the herd of swine, but that doesn't get him accepted. Then he sets out to visit the first king, where he is assaulted by the soldiers and forced into a Warrior's pose—without being able to access the Lover aspect of the archetype's balanced form.

In contrast, at the second king's palace, the king and his daughter's willingness to welcome Hans allows him to take a step toward acceptance, allowing him to risk nakedness and openness and become a Warrior-Lover. The princess, for her part, has enough courage, duty, and free will to motivate both these qualities. In common with Hans, she is a Warrior-Lover, who has been waiting to be coaxed forward.

When two people meet who are on the verge of discovering the best part of themselves in this way, their relationship can unleash the vital powers that have been waiting for a very long time to find expression in the wider world. Both partners blossom in ways that seem astounding, miraculous, and transformative. When this happens, they become unrecognizable to those who knew them in earlier days. Hans's father doesn't recognize him, at all. To some extent Hans's father never knew the true Hans; all he could see was the outside. Seen this way, the tale is moving, inspiring, and a most useful lesson about what to look for in love.

The tales "Hans the Hedgehog," in this chapter, and "Allerleiruah," in the previous chapter, are worth discussing in this way because they are basically the same sort of tale about psychic healing—in one case, for a young man, and in the other case, for a young woman. Casual readers tend to think that fairy tales are always to do with how young women should be patient and suffer, while princes prance around the place, fully formed and perfect. This has led to the charge of sexism. I think we can see from these two tales that it would require considerable ignorance of what actually occurs in the tales to make such a generalization.

## CHAPTER 9

# "The Three Feathers"

## The Descent Into the Self

The tales frequently give us a slow-witted character, sometimes nicknamed "Simpleton" or "Dummling" ("little stupid one"), who wins out in the end. Just as frequently, though, we see tales about simpleton characters who are clearly ridiculous and cannot be seen any other way.

For example, "Clever Elsie" (Tale No. 34) may be a story that tickled the sense of humor of audiences in bygone ages, but most of us find it induces only wincing these days. Elsie is so simple, and so easily confused, that when she wakes up in a field in which she has taken a nap she isn't sure who she is. So she runs home to ask if Elsie is at home. Her husband is ready for her and answers that Elsie is at home. So Elsie, not knowing who she is, runs out of the village and "has not been seen since." A similar tale, "Hans in Luck" (Tale No. 83), hinges upon a number of disastrous trades. Hans gives away a huge lump of gold (his entire earnings for seven years) for a horse. He then consecutively trades the horse for a cow, the cow for a pig, the pig for a goose, and the goose for a stone grinding wheel. Finally, the grinding stone falls in the well, releasing Hans from all burdens and he is satisfied at last.

It's hard to know what to make of some of these tales, and that in itself is a clue. Clearly, listeners at the time liked to laugh at the foolishness of others—that is only human nature. For this reason, we have tales that show silly people doing things no sensible peasant would do. "Hans in Luck," "Clever Hans" (Tale No. 32), "The Golden Goose" (Tale No. 64), and "Clever Elsie" are all examples of this, and there are others. There are also tales of simple or stupid characters who do prosper, for no praiseworthy reason. "Hans Married" (Tale No. 84) is an example of that, as is "Gambling Hänsel" (Tale No. 82) and "The Thief and his Master" (Tale No. 68).

The third group is made up of simpletons who are despised but do the right thing in the end. In this group the simplicity of the character, who is often a third son, is to be seen in a different way—namely, as purity of heart and innocence.

The tale of "The Three Feathers" (Tale No. 63), which we will be examining in this chapter, falls into this third group. Interestingly enough, "The Three Feathers" is placed just before "The Golden Goose," in which the simplemindedness of the protagonist is used for obvious comic effect. In "The Golden Goose," Dummling succeeds in making the princess laugh when no one else can, just by entertaining her with his goose—a goose that has various people stuck to it by a magic spell.

"The Three Feathers" offers another way of viewing the central character. A king has three sons, one of whom, the youngest, is called Simpleton. The king is unsure which of the sons should inherit his kingdom, so he sets them a test: they must find the most beautiful carpet in the world.

In order to decide which direction to search for the carpet, the king blows three feathers in the air and each son agrees to follow a feather no matter which direction it takes. One feather flies east, one flies west, and one falls directly to the ground. Two of the brothers then travel east and west respectively; but the third, Simpleton, must remain where he is.

Simpleton sits down feeling sad about his somewhat more limited options. Then, at his feet, he sees a trapdoor covering a hole and climbs down. Inside the hole he finds a huge toad, surrounded by many little toads, who asks him what he wants. Simpleton requests the most beautiful carpet in the world. The toad fulfils his wish and gives him the carpet. Returning to the surface, Simpleton offers the carpet to his father, who is delighted because the other two brothers have merely got some coarse handkerchiefs from shepherds' wives they have met.

The king declares the simpleminded youngest son will have the kingdom, but the other two brothers demand another test. This time, the task is to find the most beautiful ring. The feathers are blown in the air as before, with the same result. Once more, Simpleton climbs down into the hole, meets the toad, makes his request, and receives the finest of rings. The brothers don't try very hard and return with old rusty carriage rings, which means the victory goes to the youngest again.

Inevitably, the two older brothers demand a third test. This time, the test is to find the most beautiful maiden. Once again the king blows the feathers in the air, and once again, the result is the same as the previous two times. The youngest son climbs down into the hole, meets the toad, and makes his request. On this occasion, he is given a hollow yellow turnip and six mice and is told to place one of the small toads in the turnip, whereupon the turnip and mice become a carriage and horses and the toad a beautiful maiden. This is an echo of Perrault's version of "Cinderella," in which a fairy godmother does the same thing with a pumpkin. The youngest son duly returns to the surface with the carriage and horses and the beautiful maiden.

Since his brothers have brought back only the first peasant women they have met, the king declares the simpleminded youngest son has won. Yet again, the older brothers demand one more test—that the two peasant women they have brought back to the king should be made to jump through a ring hung in the center of the hall. The king agrees. The peasant women jump through the ring but fall and break their arms and legs in the process; however, the beautiful maid who had once been a toad jumps through the ring effortlessly, thereby confirming Simpleton's victory before the entire court.

Any number of objections could be leveled at this tale. The most obvious is that the simpleminded youngest son does not actually do anything, since he is merely given what he wants. How does that make him fit to be a king? We are also told that, once he has become king, the youngest son "ruled wisely." What is the source of that wisdom, then?

Well, for a start, we might note that the simpleminded youngest brother has a far better attitude than his brothers. A task is set, and he truly wants to do his best. His brothers don't even try. They get handkerchiefs from the first shepherds' wives they meet. Shepherds tending their sheep were frequently away from home for long periods of time, so shepherds' wives were sometimes seen as easy objects of seduction.

This wouldn't matter so much if we didn't have the disturbing information that, when faced with the third test, the brothers choose random peasant women as their version of the most beautiful maiden in the world. There's a sense that not only do these brothers not care about the task they've been set but that they use any excuse to go out and run around with rather low-status women, presumably in search of sex.

Similarly, when it comes to the second test, as far as the older brothers are concerned, a ring is just a rusty old carriage ring. But a ring, especially a very beautiful one, is what one gives to a valued friend or perhaps a future spouse. The king's ring and the king's seal were signs of power and prestige and were often sent with specific people as signs that the bearer had particular authority. The two older brothers don't understand any of this—they are only interested in doing things the easy way. In fact, we might conclude that they don't really seem to want the kingdom or presumably they'd try harder.

What we have, then, is a tale in which the simpleminded youngest son is blessed with purity of heart and intent, which is why he doesn't seem too successful in worldly terms. When he sees the trap door he has no hesitation in descending into the underworld, the realm of the unconscious. He isn't revolted by the toad he meets there and has no qualms about asking for what he wants—a gift that he just as quickly receives. Furthermore, the youngest son accepts all three tests and makes no protest about climbing back down the hole to visit the toad each time; nor does he protest the third gift of the turnip and mice, even though he doesn't immediately know what they mean.

Simpleton has one important quality: he wants to do the best he can. He's the one who is sad when the feather gives him what seems like limited options. He recognizes, though, that there are times in life when we must start where we are and pay attention to what is happening, even if it means we must descend deep into the self. The unconscious, represented by the underground cave inhabited by the toad, is where all the real riches of the psyche are to be found. They must be brought to the surface in order for each of us to fulfil our destinies.

It is this ability that sets the simpleminded youngest son apart. It is the lesson we all need to assimilate, so that we work not from the intellectual arrogance characteristic of the other brothers, who assume they're cleverer than anyone else, but from a place of deep thought and humility. When we feel ourselves blocked by events, we must go deeper to find our best strategy to deal with the situation.

The final piece of the tale, in which the young woman who had been a toad jumps effortlessly through the ring, is not coincidental. What it signifies is that the test is something that is true to her original nature. She doesn't have to try to be anything she is not in order to win. The peasant women, by contrast, try so hard that they break their arms and legs.

As with so many tales, when characters try something and can only do it by hurting themselves, it's a good indication that this is not the right person for the job. To understand this, consider the stepsisters in "Cinderella": they can squeeze into the golden slipper only if they cut chunks off their feet. Closer to home, we could think of those people who do their jobs well but at considerable cost in terms of spiritual effort and physical exhaustion. The man who holds down his hi-tech job and turns up each day to his cubicle may be capable, but he may also have to brace himself every day with antidepressants, alcohol, or drugs so that he can bear to face his life. He's not a bad person. He just isn't right for that job. The effortless leap of the toad/woman is an indication that the youngest son is in a place where he naturally fits.

The point, of course, is that being able to descend into that dark world of the unconscious, to accept the riches that it has, and to bring them back to the surface—these are what growth is about. Mere learning and street smarts are what the other brothers have. The youngest brother becomes worthy of the kingdom not because he can win the competitions but because he can learn to trust that other world. When we go through difficulties and personal disasters, if we choose to face them squarely, something changes within us; it has nothing to do with our personal history, our academic track record, or what others may think.

The idea of descending into the unconscious is a life lesson not everyone can assimilate and understand, as the many tales that seem concerned with shaming the simpleminded protagonist demonstrate all too well. Most of us act and judge by the standards of everyday practicality, which may not involve a lot of introspection, and we do not stay open to the transcendent or the miraculous. That, the tale suggests, is our loss.

Ultimately, stories of this kind are not about what makes a good king, nor are they about the victories of a single character; instead, they are concerned with the ability of the reader or listener to access that rich inner space within. In order to be Monarchs in our own lives, we must recognize that not everything is about the material world, and when we are stumped as to the way forward—as the simpleminded hero is—it does not matter whether we are intelligent: thinking will not solve some problems, but being in touch with the riches of the unconscious will.

And what are we to make of the king asking the sons to find and bring to him the most beautiful carpet, ring, and woman? Any artist will confirm that there can never be anything that everyone agrees is the "most beautiful" carpet, ring, or woman; all we can ever do is discover beauty that meets our own standards, then usher it into the world. Totally unselfconsciously, painters I have known have occasionally said things like, "I've just done the most beautiful painting." What they mean is that *they* see it as beautiful, something that's been given to them to bring into the world. It's not about them; it's about the beauty.

Equally, advertising executives may spend a fortune on surveying who is "the most beautiful" model or what is the most appealing product, but I think we can see that the majority vote is not what's at issue in the tale of "The Three Feathers." The other two brothers seem to think they can simply assert what beauty is and get away with it. In fact, they seem to be very successful at bullying the king. They persuade him three times to run the contest again, despite the evidence being against them.

This sort of behavior will be familiar to many of us from our experiences in meetings with work colleagues and from observing politicians at work; however, the fact that one person insists that something has to be a certain way does not make it the right way. Nevertheless, committees and governments the world over have been dominated by people who have nothing more to recommend them than loud voices and an unwillingness to be reasonable.

The Grimm brothers' tales indicate we must not take this information lightly. In "The Three Feathers" and in other tales, especially "The Gnome" (Tale no. 91) and "The Water of Life" (Tale No. 97), the brothers don't just want to win the kingdom; they want to kill their brother. They feel no compunction about doing this. The term "sibling rivalry" may be so commonplace we ignore it today but this 1812 collection of folktales unhesitatingly reveals the murderous nature of family struggles for power and supremacy, especially where inheritance is concerned. It's the part of the life struggle that we'd all, perhaps, wish to ignore, but it's still a powerful lesson and very relevant today.

The older brothers, then, operate from a world that is all ego, and no wisdom, while Simpleton operates from a mindset that trusts inner processes. The tale of "The Three Feathers" is an invitation to trust that inner world.

All six archetypes can be found in the tale. The simpleminded youngest son is an Innocent, guileless and straightforward, who, when his feather is blown into the air and goes nowhere is mocked and left on his own to decide what to do, thereby becoming an Orphan. When his brothers head out on journeys to find the objects the king asks of them, our simple hero is sad. In one sense, he'd like to go exploring the world, too, but he has to stay at home. This leads him to explore the inner world, as a Pilgrim. He shows no fear of the toad, which indicates his basic courage, and presents his carpet, ring, and young woman to the king with confidence. He's doing his best to fight for what he deems worthy—the kingdom.

The youngest son passes the Warrior-Lover's most difficult test when he is offered the turnip and the toad and takes them, without understanding how they can help him. He's reached a point where even the riches of the unconscious seem to have failed him. He doesn't despair, though; he trusts. And, of course, the young woman in her carriage with the horses comes into existence at the right moment.

Sometimes, as we go through life, we reach a still point where it seems as if nothing is going to come to us. For writers, this can be the paralyzing condition of writer's block. The "what am I going to say?" panic of the writer, the speaker, or the teacher is indeed frightening, especially if that is how one makes one's living. At such moments, we just have to let go of our wish to control, to trust that something will appear, and carry on as before. Of course, if we're in this sort of situation we can always find something third rate to fill the gap. That's exactly what the other two brothers do.

To illustrate what I mean, let me offer an example. Many years ago, I knew a man who told me that he used to go and see his girlfriend every evening, and that before he went he'd think of two or three topics they could talk about. He did this every night for several years. He was so afraid they'd run out of conversation that he scripted his life. That's one way to deal with uncertainty; but as the tale tells us, sometimes we have to just let events take their course, trusting that they'll work out one way or another and that staying authentic is what is most important.

This gives us an insight into the simpleminded son's actions. In life, the way we love others is the way we love ourselves. Simpleton is honest and does his best, and it's clear he loves his father, respects the tasks that will lead to the choosing of a new king, and that in respecting this process he loves others. His brothers are all about pretense and disrespect. They grasp at easy answers rather than taking the time to find a solution that comes from a more thoughtful approach. They may be equipped with large egos, but they don't actually love themselves or anyone else.

A king, if he is to be the embodiment of the Monarch archetype, has to love and respect all his subjects equally and not work from the place of ego. That would be a good brief description of the youngest brother. He has never lost contact with the inner purity of the Innocent archetype, the ability to love and trust others, as well as himself. He's a whole human being. He may not be the first choice if we want a leader today—these days we seem to reward the opportunist and the smooth operator—but he will be a real man, an authentic individual. It's a theme we've seen recently in such movies as *Forrest Gump* and *Being There*, where the main figure's purity of heart is what makes everything possible.

In some ways, the story asks why it is we don't have more room in our world for such pure and elevated souls. We can answer that by saying that universally beloved individuals who have transformed society—people like Nelson Mandela, Martin Luther King Jr., Mahatma Gandhi, and Mother Teresa—are in short supply but they still exist. We should remember also that each of these inspirational reformers was written off as a hopeless case at some point; each was derided and disrespected and seen as a fool. I don't suppose the two brothers in the tale gave their younger sibling much respect, either, even after he was king.

Some of us may find it hard to relate to the descent into the deep realm of the unconscious and the acceptance of what is there that lies at the heart of "The Three Feathers," so let me offer an example that relates specifically to this tale.

A female colleague wanted to change her life and find another job and career. Her tendency was to approach this in a slightly haphazard way, grasping at possibilities without having thought them out fully. The restaurant business appealed to her and, at one point, she began negotiations to start a café. Unfortunately she hadn't begun to think through what it meant to open and run such a place and, subsequently, became disillusioned and abandoned the plan. She then dreamed up an idea for marketing kids' clothes, became very excited by it, began manufacturing things, and expended a huge amount of energy trying to get the project off the ground. She then, suddenly, dropped the idea before the project was fully underway because she had decided to start a home-decorating business. This sort of uncentered activity went on for a while. It seems reminiscent of the older brothers in this tale: they grasp at what seems easiest.

What became more and more obvious from this woman's behavior was that she had never taken the time to look deeply inside herself and see who she was. If she had been able to do so, it would have been possible for her to see that her desire for an "easy answer" was a masking action. In her heart, she didn't truly believe she could be herself and have a successful, solvent career over a lifetime. She felt that the best she could do was to have a small success now and then. So she tended to create drama in her world, specifically so that she wouldn't have to go down through that trapdoor, meet that large ugly toad, and ask it for help.

Without dwelling on the specific details, this woman was constantly bouncing from failed activity to failed activity because, deep down, she wanted someone to rescue her. In this she was yearning after the father who deserted the family, whom she hoped would come back and make everything right again. Well, the absent father wasn't coming back. If this woman had been able to slow down and look inside herself, she'd have been able to confront this sad fact, and by recognizing it, make the correct decisions about her life.

The "ugly toad" is merely our reluctance to encounter our own neediness—that's why it's ugly. We can take that gift of real insight and say, now I know what I must do to have a reasonably successful life. For the woman, the lesson would be to stop expecting a rescue. If she could bring that unconscious wish to the surface she could "own" it, see that there's no disgrace in it, take that valuable lesson, and start to rescue herself.

The genius of the tale of "The Three Feathers" is that it gives us three figures who represent what is happening in one person's mind. The random and overexcited two brothers seem to overpower the centered youngest brother, just as this woman's frantic activities drowned out the authentic part of herself. Thus the tale shows us the problem and also its solution—if we care to look.

This brings us back to the two older brothers. Their attempts to win the kingdom for themselves are contemptible. They expend neither thought nor energy on what they bring as their expressions of personal effort. They seem to think that Dad will just give them everything. Doesn't that remind us a little of the example of the woman I just gave? The brothers' inability to reflect on their situation is their problem. They've never been to the depths, so they have no personal richness to offer. They don't seem to know what motivates them, so they don't even know the parts of themselves they can't yet "own." The tale asks us, the readers, which parts of our own lives we don't, as yet, "own." They will show themselves in the slightly out-of-control things we may find ourselves doing, and they may destroy our ambitions if we don't pay attention.

## CHAPTER 10

# "The Skillful Huntsman"

## Controlling the Passions

The tale of "The Skillful Huntsman" (Tale No. 111) offers us a number of fascinating possibilities, but it's not a well-known tale, so we'll need to go over the plot.

A young man trained as a locksmith becomes disillusioned and decides to retrain as a huntsman. In his choice of new career, we can already see the shift from a city-based life, which has to do with locking up and protecting wealth, to a more outdoors-oriented rural existence, in which the young man will have to survive by taking advantage of what he can find in the natural world. In this way the mythic dimensions of the tale are placed before us right away.

The young huntsman serves his apprenticeship. Before he heads out on his own his master gives him an air gun, which ensures he will always hit his prey. This could be an updated version of a crossbow, but for the sake of the plot it is a weapon that is accurate and absolutely quiet.

As he walks through the dark forest, night overtakes him, and he makes his bed up in a tree to avoid the wild beasts. Seeing a light a long way off, he notes its direction and throws his hat on the ground, so that he will be able to follow the straight line from the tree trunk to his hat and thence reach the light. This detail of woodsmanship helps us to see the huntsman not as a person who is lost, as in so many other tales, but as someone who is competent at his craft.

The huntsman discovers that the light comes from a fire built by three giants, over which they cook their food. When the young man shoots the food out of their mouths the giants are impressed enough to ask him to accompany them on an adventure to capture a princess. They need his quiet and deadly accurate marksmanship to kill the small dog that guards the castle.

The huntsman sets out with the giants, crosses the lake, and kills the dog, using his silent air gun. With everyone in the castle still asleep, the huntsman enters the fortress. First, he finds a sword with the king's name on it and a note stating that whosoever uses the sword will kill every adversary. Next, the huntsman locates the princess, a girl so innocent and pure that he feels he just can't hand her over to the giants. Then he catches sight of her slippers: the left slipper has her name embroidered on it; the right is embroidered with the name of her father. Choosing between the two, the huntsman decides to take the right one, leaving the left. The princess also has a scarf: this time, her name is embroidered on the left and her father's name on the right. Again, choosing between the two, the huntsman cuts out the father's name on the right, leaving the princess's name on the left. Finally, the huntsman notices the princess is stitched into her night gown, so he cuts a small piece off it and leaves.

These are odd actions but, in each case, the huntsman leaves the princess's name on her clothes and does not harm her. By taking the items with the father's embroidered name, the tale seems to be indicating that the huntsman is now releasing her from her father's power—a hint that is borne out also by his possession of the sword with her father's name on it. A large phallic silver sword, that can kill anything, is a pretty impressive masculine symbol, after all.

Thus prepared, the huntsman motions to the giants to come into the castle through a hole in the wall, and as each one puts his head through, he grabs its hair, pulls, and cuts off its head. Cutting out the tongues as trophies, the huntsman then decides to return home to his father. He does all this without waking anyone in the castle, nor does he think he needs any reward for his actions. True, he takes the sword, but, as the note tells us, it is as if he was supposed to do so. He is, symbolically, taking possession of his masculine power.

In the morning the castle awakens, and the king sees the dead giants and demands to know who is responsible. The ugly one-eyed captain of the guard takes the credit for the deed, whereupon the king insists his daughter must marry him. The princess refuses outright and is told by the king that, as punishment for her disobedience, she must take off her royal clothes and don pauper's garb and earn her living selling pots in the marketplace. The princess dutifully takes up her place in the market with her pots, but the king arranges to have carts run over her wares and destroy them. She then begs for more money to buy more pots, but neither her father nor the potter will agree to this. Again, the king orders the princess to marry the captain and, when she again refuses to do so, decrees that she must set up a hut and cook free food for anyone who wants it.

Hearing of the maiden who cooks food for everyone for free, the huntsman thinks she'll suit him nicely as a wife, since he has no money. The huntsman goes to see her and is delighted by what he sees. The princess, in turn, sees the sword with her father's name on it and asks how he got it. When she hears the tale, and sees the giants' tongues he has carried with him, she is overjoyed, and takes him to meet her father. When the huntsman produces the slipper and the fragments of cloth he has cut off, the proof that he saved everyone in the castle is too strong to deny, and the king agrees that he should marry his daughter. Delighted, the happy couple attends a feast in the castle. There, the ugly captain is asked by the king what he would do, in his place, to punish someone who has lied about such a deed as killing giants. The captain declares that such a person should be "torn in pieces," thereby writing his own death warrant.

This tale contains a number of factors that make it even more interesting than some of the others. For instance, the huntsman doesn't claim the princess right away; in fact, he has to come back and be charmed by her in her more humble role as cook, which lets us know that he's not just after her money. It also lets us see that he is attracted by who she is, rather than by her rank. Similarly the princess has to work at lowly trades, for no reward, because she refuses the captain. She doesn't take the easy way out. Her very obduracy is seen as a virtue, since she will not do something that repels her—namely, marry someone she hates. Her courage and sense of principle is matched by the huntsman's daring, since he's not afraid of the giants and he decides to do the right thing by not abducting the princess. They mirror each other.

But one detail here is interesting: the huntsman starts out as an opportunist. He likes the idea of grabbing the princess from her castle, and even though we can't know what the giants intend, we can assume it won't be benign. In fact, it looks as if this is code for kidnap and rape. When the huntsman is moved by the princess's innocent loveliness, and the fact that she's been stitched into her nightdress, which argues sexual chastity, he decides to act in a moral way. Notice that he's in charge of that large silver sword, which suggests the sexual power he could wield if he chose, just as the king whose name is on the sword later tries to use coercive power over his daughter, also for sexual purposes. He wants her to marry the captain, so he presumes to be in charge of her sexuality. The huntsman could have carried her off or could have sexually abused her; but he chooses the moral course and instead he kills her would-be abusers.

Here, it is useful to recall that the huntsman in the tale must cross a lake to reach the castle. Crossing a lake or a river requires a boat—a quite different experience from walking. If he were on foot, the huntsman could stumble across the castle unintentionally. Crossing the lake to reach it, however, requires a positive effort. Symbolically, we could say that our huntsman has to make a conscious effort to cross the lake to reach a land that is bounded by sleep.

It isn't the river Styx exactly, which the dead must cross to reach the Underworld of classical Greek mythology—although the small dog the huntsman kills is reminiscent of Cerberus, the three-headed dog who guards Hades. The similarity may be intended as a comic allusion to mythology, or perhaps it symbolizes that the huntsman is invading a realm that is actually a dream state. In the castle, we notice, everyone is asleep.

The question then becomes: how will the huntsman relate to this strange world? Will he respect it? The giants of unbridled greed and lawless passions are a strong inducement to do otherwise. As we've seen, the huntsman has entered the dark forest, crossed the lake, entered the castle, and found his way to the bedroom of the sleeping princess. In some ways, he has reached the stillpoint at the center of the castle and, therefore, at the center of himself.

The deeper meaning of the tale now begins to unfold. We can see it as a journey of both the huntsman and the princess, in which they each encounter their opposite, repressed self. The repressed aspect of the self is a natural result of socialization. When we grow and begin to identify ourselves as either men or women we do so, largely, by repressing those aspects of ourselves that do not fit the sexual identity we are taking on. So, boys become boys by doing male activities and also by rejecting certain aspects they consider to be girlish. Girls do the same thing with "male" activities, and there are, obviously, many variants of this balancing act. The trouble is that this can cut us off from these rejected aspects of who we are, and part of our life task is to recover them from this "shadow self" and allow those qualities back into our lives. For men, the repressed female qualities are called the *anima*; for women, the male qualities are called the *animus*.

The huntsman, for example, has a very male job—hunting and killing animals. We're told he's deliberately chosen this job and is very good at it. He also has no trouble joining those male and unruly kidnappers, the giants. In fact his male forcefulness is out of balance with his softer, "female" side, and he needs to rediscover mercy and compassion.

Seeing the tale in this way, we can understand that when the huntsman descends to the deep part of the unconscious, symbolized here first by the dark forest, and then by the castle, he descends into the shadow self to meet his anima. On the way, he will certainly encounter those powerful and lawless forces that he has repressed or denied. Sexual desires are definitely among these. In the tale, the huntsman joins forces with giants—storybook figures who are famous for their rough and uncontrollable urges—but instead of giving in to these tendencies, the huntsman realizes that he has to control them. This is shown when the huntsman finds the sword with the king's name written on it. Taking hold of it he encounters an invincible power, for the sword will kill anyone he uses it on.

This can be seen as a symbol of what happens when we reach deep inside ourselves—we find we possess great power that can be used for good or evil. In this case, the huntsman has found the capacity to murder. Remember, the huntsman is already used to killing animals, so it's not a huge step for him to become careless of other lives as well. This anarchic urge has to be faced and controlled, and this is exactly what the huntsman does. He chooses to use this power wisely and morally in order to defeat the giants. He can only do this, though, because he has been moved by the sight of the sleeping princess. He has seen his anima, the softer, feminine part of himself that he has buried and ignored until now, and he has felt its strength. He doesn't wake her, though. It's almost as if he's afraid to acknowledge that part of himself fully.

When he takes the princess's slipper with her father's name on it and removes her father's name from the scarf he is doing something that is symbolically very interesting, also. By taking away the embroidered name of her father he leaves her with just her own name. He is, therefore, setting her, his anima, free to be herself. Since she is stitched into her night gown, this suggests her sexual unavailability and lets us know of her virginity and chastity. But it also lets us know that she is imprisoned by those who want to keep her just the way she is. After all, anyone who has been stitched into anything can't take it off very easily, and must have agreed to be stitched into it in the first place.

The huntsman cuts off a small corner of her gown, symbolically showing her that there is a way to freedom. And, as we see, she wakes up and refuses her father's order to marry the one-eyed captain. The quiet, submissive Daddy's girl is not about to have the most intimate part of herself, her sexual identity, imposed on her and become the wife of someone she detests. Just as the huntsman discovers his compassionate, "feminine" aspect, the princess discovers her own determined and more "masculine" aspect. Each has set free a vital aspect of the other.

When the two meet again the huntsman sees her as merely a humble cook, and he likes what he sees. Since her task as a cook is to prepare and give away food for free he sees in her the compassionate and nurturing aspect of who she is. She's generous and patient, even though her circumstances are humble. Just as he was generous in not kidnapping her and then killing the giants, for no reward, so is she acting on her principles, also for no reward. The huntsman doesn't at first realize she's the same princess he once saw. In fact, she's the one who asks about the sword he carries, which of course allows the entire sequence of events to be reconstructed. This makes it possible for them to go to the king to explain what really happened, using the giants' tongues in the huntsman's bag as proof of him having killed them, and this explanation then allows them to marry.

We can understand the meaning of this if we consider that the huntsman has met his anima, which has permitted him to think in terms of marriage and companionship rather than kidnapping and ransom. When a man has met his anima, he is less likely to be confused about the type of woman he wishes to marry. If we think in terms of Jungian psychology, if one hasn't met one's anima (or animus, if one is a woman), then those unexamined attributes of femininity (or masculinity) that we have buried deep within us will be projected onto the first convenient figure who appears, regardless of whether this figure actually has those attributes. This is what happens with infatuation, where the individual cannot see the real person because the projection is so strong.

Often enough we can witness this sort of infatuation in those around us. Sometimes we meet a couple and find ourselves saying, "What can she possibly see in him?" And the question is a good one, because sometimes the person doesn't see what actually is there but only what she wants to see, based on her own confusions. What this means is that those who have not made the descent into the self, and who have not encountered the animus/anima, have a tendency to idealize what a life partner should be and clothe that image in whatever features the culture currently deems fashionable. On the other hand, if one has come to terms with one's anima, as the huntsman has, then one will see the qualities one admires and needs only when they actually are present, no matter how humble the other person may seem. This is precisely what the huntsman does. He recognizes that there is something in the princess that resonates in him, even though he thinks she's a cook.

On the part of the princess, the same thing applies. She hasn't seen her animus in the same way the huntsman has seen her, simply because she was asleep at the time. What she recognizes when she sees the sword, the slipper, and the fragments of cloth, though, is the person whose symbolic actions freed her from her status as her father's property, complete with embroidered name labels. The huntsman's actions wake her up to the full awareness of her selfhood, that same selfhood that then allows her to reject both her father's male tyranny over her, and the one-eyed captain.

And here is the point of this rather complex symbolism. When we discover these repressed parts of ourselves, we find that it is we who have repressed them; therefore, we are the only ones who can set ourselves free. In the tale, once the huntsman does this he becomes moral, and his small trophies are permanent reminders to himself of what he's witnessed. He knows he has a tender and moral side. This is a major developmental point for young males, and the tale lets us see this. The princess, on her part, discovers the courage to reject the captain and to keep on rejecting him.

The tale, then, sets up a duality: the lawless urge of the huntsman has to be tamed, but the rebellious urge of the princess has to be respected. In each case, it is the natural feeling as to what is right that has to be honored. This is an important distinction because the king's very male desire to humiliate his daughter is certainly not in any sense right or moral. We have, therefore, several sets of strong urges to consider: the initial urge of the huntsman not to be a locksmith; his urge to be an opportunist with the giants; and his subsequent desire to control that urge when he sees the princess. Then we have the king's desire to retain power over his daughter; the daughter's rejection of that power; and finally the cynical opportunism of the captain, which is all about the male ego and exploitation.

The captain is very much like the giants because he's an opportunist and he doesn't alter his purpose or change his mind, and those who don't change their minds in this tale wind up dead. This tale, then, deals with male urges—the huntsman, the king, the giants, the captain—and these come into conflict with the urge to mercy and compassion that is represented by the princess giving away free food. The tale comes to a happy conclusion when the male urges are tamed and the female urges are respected.

In terms of archetypes, this tale is well balanced. The huntsman is a Pilgrim as he goes on his quest, but when he sees the sleeping princess he makes a moral choice that involves courage. In this way, he transitions to the Warrior-Lover archetype. He's not afraid to fight for what he sees as right and worthy, and he doesn't ask for or want any reward. His moral decision, one might say, makes him invincible, as symbolized by the magic sword.

The princess, with her monogrammed clothing, is the property of the king, but when she refuses his orders she becomes an Orphan, ejected from the palace, and when she takes up selling pots we could say she's exploring other ways to live, this time as a Pilgrim. When that fails she is forced to become a cook, and she persists for some time in what is for her a degrading situation, showing courage and devotion to an ideal of what love and marriage should be. She's fighting for the right to be herself and is a Warrior-Lover at this point.

This is when she meets the huntsman again. Notice that she is the one who asks about the sword—there is no shy running away, such as we see with Cinderella. The princess's questions allow her to identify the huntsman not just as the man who killed the giants but as a fellow Warrior-Lover—someone who does what's right because it's right, not because it's profitable. They are now at the same archetypal level of development, so they can, rightly, be a match for each other.

We might say that these two Warrior-Lovers are the real thing, whereas the captain, who has been a warrior, and thinks of himself as a lover, has only the outer appearance of the archetype, not the inner value. The princess's rejection of the captain, seen in this way, is a rejection of the same sexual opportunism that the huntsman had to control in himself. They've each learned the same lessons.

Had the huntsman and the princess simply been married at the time the giants were killed, it would have been convenient for the story but too soon in developmental terms, since the princess would have had no chance to find out who she is or what she believes in. When they marry at the end of the tale, they are ready to become a future Monarch pair, and it is their knowledge of, and control of, the dark urges of the human psyche that will ensure they can be enlightened rulers of the country.

The tale is important because it shows the deep lawless urges of the psyche and demonstrates how these have to be understood, held in check, and even combatted. Which of us hasn't felt the desire to do something lawless because we felt we could get away with it? The giants are all appetite—they are chomping on a whole ox when we first see them—and these massively powerful figures have put themselves beyond the law, as they think.

In case we think this is all rather theoretical, we need only to look to recent history. One example that springs to mind is the recent abuse scandals of the Catholic Church, where priests have been convicted of sexual misconduct with children. Those in authority must sometimes feel very tempted to exploit a situation where others are powerless, and where all they have is their own sense of what is right. A priest is a larger-than-life figure in any community, a giant among men, one might say. And just as priests have abused power, so have college professors, Buddhist masters, yogic gurus, politicians, and others. The situation is too common to be ignored.

The value of this tale lies in what it can tell us about this struggle. Like all such tales, it can underscore what the struggle is, and how to get past it. Because the tales are brief, they don't attempt to convey the emotional turmoil that may actually be involved in the actions described. Yet what they lose in emotional appeal, they more than make up for in terms of clarity.

If we are to be happy in love, the tale suggests, we first have to give up our posturing (the huntsman's friendship with the giants), then we have to give up our projections and unearth the qualities behind those projections. We can only do that by descending into the self and seeing and acknowledging the sleeping power of our idealized images of manhood or womanhood. Then, when we return to the conscious world, we will find it much easier to identify the person who corresponds to the qualities that image conveys.

An example might help here. A female colleague of mine used to date young men who looked very youthful and innocent because she said what she wanted was someone who was "innocent," in the sense of not being devious. What she wound up with was younger men who exploited her idealism, then left her. She had to learn the difference between the outer appearance and the inner quality she sought. That is the difference between a projection that becomes an infatuation and a genuine connection with the need expressed in the unconscious. Men often do the same thing when they are attracted to younger women—they confuse the outer appearance with the inner qualities.

The story of "The Skillful Huntsman" can be seen as a tale of greater power and scope than either "Little Snow-White" or "Little Briar-Rose." In those two tales, the male protagonist (the prince) finds the girl asleep or in a state of suspended animation and brings her back to life, whereupon they are married. "The Skillful Huntsman" is more vital because the woman in this story is an active participant in her own development and in the huntsman's development, too, in ways that are not fully considered in the other two tales.

"Little Snow-White" and "Little Briar-Rose" are alike in their titles as well as their stories, which may be why they are placed close together in the collection, at Tales No. 50 and 53. They are about, in large part, the maturation of girls to women who are ready to be married. The tale of "The Skillful Huntsman," on the other hand, is about the maturation of women to wives and men to husbands and about how the two encounter each other. In examining the way men and women choose each other as mates, we enter a more complex discussion. It's the difference between a story of preparation and a story about the next stage.

Interestingly, that "next stage" is what was removed from the movie tale of "Cinderella," when the interplay of Cinderella searching for the prince and the prince searching for Cinderella was so drastically simplified by Walt Disney Pictures. It's not until we get to "The Glass Coffin" (Tale No. 163) in the Grimm collection that we see these same themes presented as strongly, and in such a complete way. In all these stories, as well as "The Golden Bird" (Tale No. 57), as we will see in Chapter 12, a sleeping princess figures prominently; but "The Skillful Huntsman" provides by far the most subtle use of this motif.

## CHAPTER 11

# "The Two Kings' Children"

## Families and Forgetting

This tale (Tale No. 113) is a long one and combines several elements that appear in other tales, so one could be mistaken for thinking it a mixture of one or more tales. The broad outlines of the story are as follows:

At the age of sixteen, a prince is told that he will be killed by a stag. One day, out riding in the woods and chasing a stag, suddenly he sees a "great tall man" who drags him off to a king's palace.

At the king's palace, the prince is immediately set the task of keeping watch over the king's three daughters. He is told that he must remain awake all night because the king will come back every hour to check that he's properly guarding that night's designated princess. Fortunately for him, the eldest daughter decides to help him out by ordering her statue of St. Christopher to answer the king whenever he appears, and the young prince gets a good night's sleep on the floor. This action is repeated by each of the daughters, each of whom has a similar talking St. Christopher statue, each one larger than the previous one.

The king then sets the prince another series of tests. On the first day, he orders him to cut down a huge forest; on the second day, he orders him to clean out and rebuild a large fish pond; and on the third day, he orders him to clear a mountain of briars and build a castle on the top, fully furnished. On each occasion the prince is given glass implements to use, which break as soon as he uses them. Luckily, the prince receives help from the youngest princess, who has set her sights on him for a husband. She takes him his lunch every day, and seeing him looking sad—for he believes he cannot do the tasks and save his life—waits until he takes a nap, then bangs her knotted handkerchief on the ground. Immediately an army of little "earth men" appear and promptly do the day's task. Each evening, when the bell strikes six o'clock, the task is done.

The tasks in themselves have some relevance. They involve clearing land and getting firewood, providing clean water and all kinds of fish, which looks a lot like the providing of drink and food, and all that is necessary for the creation of a home. In fact, the tasks look very much like the sorts of proof of intent a bride's father would request of a future son-in-law: Do you have a decent place for my daughter to live? Can you earn a living? Do you have utilities and decent plumbing? The difference is that the king wants the prince to make these items, not inherit them.

When the tasks are complete, the king sets yet another condition: that the youth cannot marry the youngest daughter until the two older daughters are married. The young couple, therefore, decides to flee. As they run away, the king pursues them, but the daughter changes the son into a briar bush, with herself as the rose at the center. The king can't understand what has happened and where they have disappeared to, so he tries to get the rose, but the briars prick him and he gives up.

The next day the king again tries to find the pair. When he reaches the spot where he thinks they are hiding, the daughter has transformed them into a church with herself as a priest in it. The king listens to the sermon and leaves. The queen, however, knows what's going on, and the next day she goes looking for the young couple herself. This time the daughter has transformed the prince into a pond with herself as a fish in it. The queen tries to capture the fish, swallowing the whole pond in the process. When she vomits it all up again, she admits defeat and gives the daughter three walnuts, telling her that they will be useful when the girl is in great need.

The young couple continues to the prince's homeland. When the castle comes into sight, the prince asks the princess to wait while he goes ahead to get a carriage for her. When he reappears at the castle he is met with great joy. He is just about to have the carriage arranged when his mother arrives and gives him a kiss, whereupon he forgets all about the waiting princess.

The princess waits for a long time and eventually takes menial work at a mill to support herself. Then, one day, she hears the king's son is due to be married, since his mother has found a suitable bride. She cracks one of the nuts, finds a beautiful dress inside, and goes to the church. There, just as the vows are about to be made, the bride sees the magnificent dress and refuses to be married until she can wear it.

The young princess makes a bargain that she will hand over the dress if she can sleep outside the groom's door for one night. This is agreed, except that someone, we're not told who, tells the servants to give the prince a sleeping draught. That night, then, when the young princess sits outside the door and tells the prince about all she has done for him, he's fast asleep. He does not hear, but the servants do.

The second day the princess again appears for the wedding, but this time her dress is even more beautiful. Again, the young princess strikes the same deal with the bride. This night, however, the servant has brought a drink that keeps the prince awake and he hears everything. He begins to recall his former life and tries to open the door, but the queen has locked it. The next day, the prince finds the princess, tells her what has happened, and asks her not to be angry with him. She now cracks the third walnut, finds an even better dress than before, and the pair are married. "The false mother and the bride had to depart," we are told.

The tale is remarkably similar to several other stories in the collection, such as "The True Bride" (Tale No. 186) and "The Drummer" (Tale No.193), in which the princess causes the tasks to be magically achieved; in each case, the parental kiss causes the young prince to forget his love, and the princess is forced to take menial work until the dresses allow her three nights of vigil outside his bedroom door.

If we look at "The Two Kings' Children" with a skeptical eye, we could say that the young princess does everything for this hopeless youth, and that she is actually humiliated by having to work in a mill scrubbing the meal tubs, then by sleeping outside his door. The message seems to be that women are to be bullied.

But this would be a reading of the tale that would throw out anything of value, so we'll have to say that the three nights the king's son watches over the king's daughters are matched by the three times when she watches over him (although the third day breaks that pattern). We'd also note the three tasks, in which the prince goes to sleep and the princess calls up the "earth men," are matched by the three days they spend fleeing. Similarly, we have one queen who tries to get the runaways back and gives the daughter the three walnuts, and this is matched, on the other side, by another queen who also has her own plans as to whom the son is to marry and tries on three occasions to thwart the pair. This formal patterning lets us know that there's something going on beyond the obvious.

So let's start at the beginning, this time looking at the tale as a mythic structure. The son is fated to be "killed" by a stag at sixteen, we are told. At sixteen, a boy is usually sexually mature, even if not emotionally mature, and a stag is certainly a figure of sexual maturity anyone could identify. The boy is not killed; however, he *is* removed from his ordinary life to undergo some tests that will lead him to marriage, and thus to sexual experience.

The start of the tale seems to tell us that we're dealing with a maturation story in which the boy must "die" to his old nature. The substitution of a "great tall man" for the expected stag is a strong hint that this tale will be about reaching manhood. The threat of death, though, puts us on warning that the failure to grow and mature is, for anyone, a serious fault. A sixteen-year-old who cannot grow up is, to all intents and purposes, not fully alive at all.

This can help us understand some other odd details. When the young man keeps guard over the daughters, he is clearly inside their rooms. That's why the king needs to shout through the door and can be fooled by St. Christopher's voice answering.

The fact that the young man sleeps seems to indicate that he's not sexually active with the other occupant, and the large speaking figure of the saint is an added precaution—because one wouldn't want to do anything immoral in front of such a creature.

Symbolically, this is the realm of sexual temptation that awaits all young people as they grow up. Will the young man be uncontrolled and leap into the bed of the first person who gives him half a chance? Well, he doesn't, but probably only because he's being closely watched. His religious scruples keep him from doing anything rash. Sometimes, that's a form of control that is both effective and necessary. The young man doesn't want to hurt the daughters, and neither do they want to hurt him. They make sure that they help him fool their father by using the talking statues, which is a gentle hint that they see how unreasonable their father is being and shrug it off.

The result of these bogus vigils is that the youngest daughter is the one who takes him his lunch each day during the next series of tests. The other daughters just aren't interested, so the youngest is forced to go. When she sees him, he is in despair over his task and refuses to eat anything, saying he's going to die anyway, so what's the point? Then, we are told, she "spoke so kindly to him" that he ate some food. We are also told that, after he's eaten, she "picks his lice"—a rather intimate piece of grooming, not exactly usual these days—and when he falls asleep (there's the sleep motif again) she calls up the "earth men" to complete his tasks.

If we wish to see this as a symbol, we might say that the youngest princess acts in a loving and comforting way toward the prince. For his part, he's not afraid to die, just sad at the prospect. This suggests courage, while the princess coaxing him to eat encourages him to think about living. In her company he relaxes enough to sleep, presumably with his head in her lap, the usual way lice are picked. Whatever else we wish to see here, it's pretty clear that there is physical acceptance and ease between these two. She encourages him to eat and not despair, they share an ease of physicality, albeit chaste, and there seems to be real sympathy between them. At such unguarded and open moments, when we feel able to be ourselves, miracles occur.

Note that the king's son doesn't ask how the youngest daughter achieved the impossible tasks he's been set, and he doesn't lie by saying he did them; he just tells the king that they are completed. The suggestion is that as the princess changes in her attitude toward him it allows her to command considerable power from the unconscious, which she uses to help him.

Let's put this in everyday terms. The young princess is surely not the first woman to coach a potential partner through the perils of the family's demands and expectations, some of which may be very exacting indeed. For example, we may not think it a big thing to warn a partner not to talk politics with our father or be sure to praise the new dining room set to please our mother, but it's the same basic loving impulse.

These little tips may not seem important, but they are the surface ripples, the slight signs of real affection, caring, and love, which when combined become a major force in a future relationship. The daughter's ability to work magic is a version of this, writ large.

Symbolically, the inadequate implements the young man is given to carry out his tasks are not accidental. The father sets an impossible task because no one can ever be quite good enough for a beloved daughter. The king just doesn't want his child to marry. The tools made of glass are perhaps suggestive of the fact that things may look like they're serviceable, but they might not actually stand the pressure of use. The young prince may look the part, but is he all appearance and no substance? The youngest princess, by having the deeds done for him, brings the kings' son face to face with his own inadequacy, and he seems to be happy not to be found out.

Obviously, though, this is not a good recipe for a successful relationship, so let's take this one step farther. These tasks are impossible. No one could do them, just as no one can ever be good enough for a possessive father's daughter, at least in the father's eyes. Yet the daughter knows differently, so she helps the son, because she recognizes that he's human, and that is a vitally important step in any romance. She doesn't idealize him; instead, she helps him, in all his frailty. What a lovely expression of acceptance that is!

The little army of "earth men" has symbolic undercurrents as well. The power of the earth itself rallies to help this pair, the depth of nature is on their side. In calling up this army, the young princess is showing that she is in contact with the deep, powerful, instinctual urge of love, and the young man accepts her gift, without question. If faith can move mountains, this is an example of it in action. This is the sort of image that is far more suggestive than can easily be spelled out in words, but it suggests the vital connection the couple shares.

When the pair runs away, the symbolism changes. They flee because they wish to marry and have been forbidden to do so until the older daughters are married. In the past this was not an unusual custom, and the young couple's decision to elope tells us about the urgency of what they feel for each other. There's a real attraction there. So when the daughter is pursued by the king and queen and transforms herself and the prince, we notice the symbolism of what they become: on the first day, the prince becomes the briar, and the princess becomes the rose; on the second day, the prince becomes the church, and the princess becomes the priest; and on the third day, the prince becomes the pond, and the princess becomes the fish.

In each case the prince is the larger environment that allows the princess to exist. They are interdependent, since they are nothing without each other, but one is the basic strength and the other is what gives the structure meaning and value. It is truly a beautiful image pattern, and it suggests the interdependent nature of love. In fact, it's such a good image sequence that it is also used in other tales. "Sweetheart Roland" (Tale No. 56) is a very similar tale that replicates this sort of image pattern, including the three days the bride has to wait outside the door.

These images tell us something important. When two people are in love and are right for each other something miraculous happens. They remain themselves, but being with the other allows the couple to be more than they were singly. An empty church is nothing special. A priest by a roadside is simply another person. Together, they become a potent force for good and for moral instruction. A pond is not un-usual, and a fish on its own will soon die; but a pond with a fish in it is a symbol of life. Similarly, a briar on its own is a sturdy but inconvenient plant that gets in every-one's way. A cut rose is delightful but will soon fade. However, a rose growing on a briar is alive and will be protected by the briar; it will eventually produce a seed pod, and more briars will come of that. We have, in each case, symbols of strength that are interdependent. When two young people bring out the very best in each other in love we have a pairing that is, indeed, astonishing.

In this tale, though, what is interesting is that the queen knows exactly what's go-ing on. That's why she tries to drink up the pond. When she can't manage to do so, she realizes that the couple's love is too big for her to deal with, too much for her to try and smother. So she gives in and blesses the union in her own way with the three magical walnuts.

When the king's son reaches home we see another mother. It's immediately obvi-ous when his mother kisses him and he forgets about his bride, that we're dealing with a controlling mother figure. Countless mothers over the centuries have discounted potential brides for their children without ever having seen them, let alone observed what the quality of the relationship might be. The son forgets his life with the prin-cess so entirely, the real magic his beloved has worked is never even mentioned. This is a real factor in our world, too, and it has caused misery to many a young couple. In popular culture, there are more than enough mother-in-law jokes to let us know about this. So, just as the daughter had to break free of her father's controlling ways, the son has to free himself from his mother's plans for him. Both the "kings' children" have a similar struggle and are almost mirror images of each other.

When the princess is able to spend the night outside the son's door we can see several things happening. The first is her devotion. The second is that we notice how another's devotion to us can be blocked out of our awareness. The prince doesn't hear her because someone (almost certainly his mother) gave orders to have his drink drugged. The scene is richly symbolic, since we can easily imagine the small voice on the other side of the door in the middle of the night asking why he's forgotten

THE TWO KINGS' CHILDREN

her—it's like something we might dream as a motif. It suggests the way our memories come back to haunt us at night, when our conscious mind is shut down and the unconscious is at work, reminding us of what we know and of what is true.

On the second night, when the prince hears the voice, he knows who it is and what she's telling him; this time, though, he's locked in his room and can't get out. That means he has to go and find her, tell her he recalls their relationship, then take the lead. No one opposes the marriage now—a sure sign that he's in charge of his own life. The prince's mother can't make him forget what he knows is true, and the princess's mother is recalled also in the use of the third, and finest, of the dresses for the wedding.

In our modern lives, we are all capable of similar actions. We forget the ease and the real magic of early relationships we may have had and find ourselves being seduced by what others expect of us, so that we choose the "suitable" partner rather than the one that feels absolutely right, and always did. We forget what we know, our deep wisdom, when there is sufficient opposition.

This family opposition comes from several directions, we notice in this story. First, the young man has to tame his own urges toward sex when he holds his three vigils, and the king, like a nosy chaperone at a teenage party, insists on making sure the young man is seemingly abiding by his rules. This is the parent who insists on the 11pm curfew but who does not bother to ask what actually happened in the hours leading up to 11pm. Perhaps the lesson here is that we all have to learn to respect and even to fear authority in the shape of the king, but we would be unwise to give in to him in important things to do with personal choices. And that's precisely why the young man decides to elope with the daughter. They're not going to wait around for years because convention dictates that the older sisters have to be married first.

Similarly, the tale suggests it is absolutely reasonable to flee and avoid the queen, but we should also be prepared to fight if we do so. The daughter is, in this way, separating herself from her mother, which is an important developmental step for any woman, and she eventually defeats her. The queen cannot "stomach" what's happening, but she can't control it, either. The couple's love proves too powerful for her.

The young man has the same struggle when he returns home. His mother may have well-meaning plans, but she's not the one who will have to live with the results. One interesting detail in the tale has the mother catch sight of the princess when she's working at the mill. She finds herself admiring her, saying, "What a fine strong girl that is! She pleases me well!" From this, we can surmise that the mother might actually approve of the woman her son has already chosen and will eventually marry, but she has other plans that prevent her from acting on the evidence right in front of her. The mother is not a bad person, nor lacking in awareness, but in this she makes a grievous mistake.

Viewed in this way, we can appreciate this tale as a subtle and important outline of the way women and men can mature and the opposition any of us may face as we do so. St. Christopher, we recall, is the saint who carried Jesus over the flood. He is the patron saint of travelers and, therefore, of transitions, where one moves from one place to the next and grows into something different along the way. His statue is in each of the girls' rooms, helping the prince to get a good night's rest. It's almost as if St. Christopher is overseeing the whole situation and allowing the safe passage to manhood and womanhood in each case.

In terms of archetypes, this tale is equally rewarding, since we can see the Orphan prince undergoing several tests—always the domain of the Pilgrim—that bring him into a loving relationship with the young princess. Each has to struggle to hold onto the other's love, and each, we might say, balances the other. The Lover and the Warrior exist in both the prince and the princess, in similar degrees, and their interdependence as signaled by the imagery of the briar and the rose, the priest and church, and the fish and the lake shows that each needs the other. In fact, each is a Lover and a Warrior fighting for what is necessary to their happiness.

An interesting detail is that the young princess seems able to perform magic, and this magic is a function of their relationship. It is unlikely that the daughter had this ability before she met the young man—if she had, then her father would not have permitted her to help him. The magic happens *because* they are together. What we see here is that, when a relationship is strong and promising, magic occurs at unusual times because the participants are able to access the Magician archetype. The purity, indeed the innocence, of the love they share shows us that they are still powerfully in contact with the Innocent's ability to love without question or hesitation. As we have seen, this is a reconnection the Magician archetype needs to make, and the young couple has this ability.

In more ordinary terms, when love grows between two people it is often astonishing what they can accomplish. Older couples will often look back on the early days of their life together and wonder how they managed to hold a job, create a career, rebuild and redecorate a home, take care of Aunt Meg, and still raise the children. In retrospect, it seems impossible, miraculous. At the time, it was just what they did. This is what the tale points toward.

But just as the couple can leap ahead in this way, they can also slip backward. The young man in the tale forgets his lover entirely when his mother takes charge of him. This is an extreme action, but it feels psychologically absolutely true. When we return to our parents after a life-changing episode in our lives, if the parents were not present to see what went on there's a strong tendency for them to see us as we were last time they saw us—before the event concerned. This can be a major source of friction for many young people as they grow up.

And that's exactly what we see with the queen. She takes charge of the prince as if he'd never been away on his extraordinary pilgrimage, and he does what so many of us tend to do: we forget what we know and we lose sight of our real wisdom when a parent treats us as less than we truly are. I see this in my teaching life. Undergraduates go home for vacations or weekends and holidays and often return infuriated because their parents have treated them as if they're fifteen again, rather than seeing the twenty-year-old or twenty-one-year-old they now are. A short span of years makes a lot of difference; parents forget that at their peril.

Occasionally, of course, young people finish college, then head back to the parental home and are, sometimes, infantilized by the experience. They become dependent and less capable than they were before. If they are to take charge of their lives again they need to be reminded of their real strengths. One hint is often not enough! Those three nights of vigils (echoed also in the "The Iron Stove," Tale No.127) are necessary to jog the individual back to self-direction—a true call to wake up and pay attention. Often this nudge comes from those of the young person's friends who have been out in the world, as the maiden has when she takes on the menial work, or from those who have made their own way. It's a telling detail, even today, and psychologically accurate.

The tale, therefore, reminds us that archetypal development is not always a smooth transition that moves ever upward, and that progress can be derailed. Luckily, the courage and persistence of the daughter, who lays siege to the bedroom door of her beloved, pays off. These qualities are definitely the Warrior-Lover's realm. The princess knows what she wants and the ego concerns about loss of dignity are simply not part of her awareness. The recognition of what she's done, and the memory of what the couple has lived through, is enough to bring the young man back from his passive Orphan phase to full Warrior-Lover status again. The "sleeping draught" that prevents him hearing his lover outside his bedroom door on the first night is an emblem of how anyone can be lulled back into the narcotic ease of Orphan status.

This is not, however, to be confused with the nap the young prince takes, when the "earth men" do the work he's supposed to do. There, he may not understand exactly how things came to pass, but he sees the results clearly enough and knows that something remarkable happens between the girl and himself, or perhaps more correctly that she makes remarkable things happen for him. There's a sense that she's always had this magic; she just hasn't had any reason to use it before now.

As we've already noticed, her father the king doesn't know about this, or he wouldn't have allowed her to help out the young man in this way. And that's the whole point. Fathers are often unaware of the wonderful qualities of their children because they've forgotten to look. The daughter who comes from a fine suburban home and turns out at college to be an organizational genius may well be a surprise to her parents. The talents never had a chance to shine until the daughter went to college, perhaps. That might be a good alternative version of the young woman in the tale. Or the daughter who may turn out to be a brilliant actress or a superb artist might never have given much hint of that in the home, where the parents were focused on other things. This is perhaps how we might explain the situation of the princess in the tale in modern terms.

It doesn't take a lot of imagination to find other examples. Among my students, I can think of the football player who was idolized for his running-back abilities, then won a scholarship to law school. This took his parents totally by surprise because they saw him only as a ball player who would build on that part of his identity as his future career. They were puzzled by their son, whom they felt they hardly knew any more.

I can also think of people who chose a significant other and blossomed as a result of being part of a partnership. Alone each person would perhaps never have been able to generate the synergy that allowed each to grow and become fully who they could be together. That's the magic the young princess accesses.

When the two young people in this tale marry, they are, therefore, already experienced in the ways of the world, and they know a thing or two about how power can be used to crush individual initiative and what needs to be done about that. Knowing this, they are ready to rule a kingdom; more importantly, though, they are ready to rule their own lives. The Monarch archetype is achieved, and the Magician's power can be accessed when the need arises.

In closing, I'll return to the start of the tale. At sixteen, the young prince is told he will be killed. He doesn't die; instead, he finds a new life. The tale applies to boys at sixteen, as well as to young women. In a more general sense, it applies to anyone breaking free of an old lifestyle dominated by parents.

## CHAPTER 12

# Beowulf and "The Golden Bird"

## The Three Tests

The Old English epic poem *Beowulf* is not one of the tales in the Grimm brothers' collection.[1] Set in Scandinavia, it was written down during Anglo-Saxon times, probably in the eighth century, which places it as early as a thousand years before the brothers were collecting folktales, so it may seem like an odd addition here. I am including it by way of comparison with the Grimm tale of "The Golden Bird" (Tale No. 57), so we can dig deeper into what is being communicated in the tales at the deepest level.

One of the things *Beowulf* can tell us is about the way we shape experience. In order to understand this, we'll have to look at the plot, then at the undercurrents at work within the plot.

In the story, Beowulf, a young fighting man, leaves his homeland of the Land of the Geats in Sweden and crosses the sea with his men. When he arrives at Heorot, the palace of King Hrothgar in Denmark, he is a form of Orphan who has become a Pilgrim and set out on a pilgrimage to help his relatives. They are suffering from the depradations of a monster called Grendel who is ravaging the countryside. Not everyone is thrilled by Beowulf's arrival—Unferth, one of Hrothgar's men, doesn't want him around at first, although others are prepared to welcome this distant relation. Gradually, he is adopted into the clan and sets the action in motion.

Beowulf becomes a hero when he defeats the monster Grendel in a hand-to-hand fight in which he rips Grendel's entire arm off. His reputation is confirmed when he kills Grendel's mother and reveals himself as a faithful fighter (a Warrior-Lover). Beowulf eventually becomes an unselfish Monarch and rules his own kingdom. At the end of the poem, he dies killing a dragon, and his example is an inspiration to everyone; so he can be seen as reaching Magician status at the end. It's important to note that in this final fight Beowulf is not alone, as he was in each of the previous fights; he has a group of men with him, of whom only Wiglaf stays the full course of the action. Beowulf, therefore, moves through the six archetypal stages in a straight-forward manner, even if his Warrior-Lover archetype is focused on love of the realm he defends rather than on love of a particular human being.

So what is it we can learn from this strange story? It tends to get discussed in a variety of ways, usually focused on the story's historical significance as one of the oldest surviving examples of epic storytelling; however, I'd like to suggest its true significance lies elsewhere.

There are three monsters, and three is a repeated pattern we've noticed through-out Grimms' tales. Like the way we tend to say "good, better, best," this three-part structure is something very basic to us and to our language. What we need to focus on is that the three struggles are particularly fearsome in this poem; therefore, there is likely to be an important truth conveyed by them.

As always, the details help to furnish the clues we need if we are to understand this pattern. Beowulf travels across the sea because he feels there is a monster for him to fight; in fact, it seems as if he senses that only he can fight it, which may be why he chooses to wrestle with Grendel rather than trust to his sword and shield as the other warriors do.

Certainly, it's an unusual choice to go hand to hand with such a monster who, we are told, is a creature left over from before the Great Flood and a relative of Cain. There's a sense that this creature from the swamp is Beowulf's personal antagonist, and so the fight has to be bare-handed, nose to nose. Beowulf rips Grendel's arm off at the shoulder, trusting to his personal strength. As if to emphasize this, in the story we notice that normal swords and shields are not tremendously successful. Beowulf's men, wearing armor, are no match for Grendel. It's the absence of armor that allows for the wrestling match to happen at all.

In addition, when Beowulf later encounters Grendel's mother, the sword Un-ferth has given him, called Hrunting, cannot cut through the dragon's skin. Even this time-honored weapon is not good enough. It takes a sword that has lain in the dragon's hoard for generations, a weapon from another age, to kill the beast. Clearly, we're in a world that is not going to follow the usual rules, and where the reassurance of normal weapons is illusory. Each monster is met, and defeated, in terms of its own standards of conduct.

If we look at this tale from a mythic point of view we'd have to ask ourselves a question: What are the monsters that exist in each of us that we have to kill? For some of us, the monsters may not seem very dangerous, but they still have to be killed.

Grendel represents the spirit of discord. He doesn't gain anything from ravaging Heorot. He just doesn't like human beings to be happy and live in peace. He is the spirit of alienation and destruction that, to some extent, we all have in us, and which we must wrestle with and defeat. Beowulf is a fearsome warrior; like all fearsome destroyers, he has to know when to use his powers productively, in a controlled fashion. That's the test we saw the Skillful Huntsman go through.

For example, when Beowulf is in the hall and tells the tale of his swimming contest with Breca, which he is asked to repeat, Unferth makes snide comments, attempting to pick a fight. In the Anglo-Saxon period, men would fight to the death over words such as Unferth speaks (even his name means "unrest"). Yet Beowulf deals with the insult graciously and firmly. He is not just a blood-thirsty hired killer, and he doesn't get upset. His restraint tells us that he's not in this fight for his ego gratification; he is focused on removing the monster. Keeping this in mind, then, we can see Beowulf's fight with Grendel as the next stage in his personal struggle to use his power wisely, and the argument with Unferth is a curtain-raiser on the action.

We can understand this in our own times by calling to mind the many great leaders who started well and became tyrannical. In Russia, Stalin the young idealist was a very different person from the older Stalin who was drunk with his own success and became one of the worst mass murderers of the twentieth century. He was not a man who had ever learned to wrestle with and defeat the lust for power. It's an extreme example, perhaps, but Beowulf faces the same temptation. The things at which we excel—our inner strengths—require us to use those abilities wisely and well. The negative aspect, the shadow, has to be met and tamed.

Beowulf meets and defeats Grendel in the dark mead hall of Heorot in the middle of the night. The setting and the fight offer a wonderful image of wrestling with the dark part of our own unconscious, of the descent into the lawless regions of the self. This is also where the poem becomes even more interesting. Once Grendel is dead, the problems plaguing the kingdom are not solved. Grendel's mother, a dragon, decides to take her revenge for her son's death. Historically, this accurately reflects the customs of Anglo-Saxon times, when the killing of a man would often start a blood feud with the immediate family that would go on for generations. The mother is Grendel's only blood kin, so Beowulf must kill her, too, to end the struggle.

Again, Beowulf takes on this task alone. He follows the dragon to the fiery lake that is her lair and he jumps in, descending to its depths, sinking for a whole day, until he finds the dragon and kills her. It's another splendid image for the descent into the self. Beowulf doesn't bring back any of the treasure, of which there are enormous heaps in the cave, which indicates he is not merely greedy or vainglorious; instead, he only brings back the remains of the destroyed sword, which melted when Grendel's mother's hot black blood poured over it, and Grendel's head.

At the level of the psyche, we can see several things happening. When we deal with our own internal monsters, there is rarely just one problem. There is the problem itself, then there is the emotional situation that brought the problem into existence; we can treat the symptom, or we can treat the disease.

In terms of my counseling practice, I can say that this tale feels psychologically true as a description of the way important conflictual material will emerge. For instance, at a certain point in the course of our conversations, the client will reach a moment at which he or she thinks all the work has been done and will say, "That's it. I've got a handle on this. I don't need to come and talk with you any more." I'm always pleased to hear this; yet, I also know that this can very often be a defense, a masking behavior for someone who does not want to go any deeper and unearth the real problem. Under those circumstances, I have to remind the client that there may be more to do. On one occasion, in fact, I had to tell the woman concerned that, although she was obviously happier than she had been, we had not dealt with at least three of the issues she had come into therapy to sort out—her miserable job, her career, and her sexless marriage.

When we grapple with our personal issues—bare-handed like Beowulf, because there are no shortcuts—we can deal with the behavior fully only if we seek the source of the behavior as well. An individual can, for example, give up drinking, but unless we've looked at why this person turned to alcohol in the first place the person is likely to take up another addictive activity. Sometimes, this can be just as bad. The point is to go deeper and sort out the root cause.

To some extent we all have the tendency to be like that—we remain in a state of avoidance as much as possible. We go to the dentist and our tooth mysteriously stops aching… until we get home. We go to see our boss or a relative, and the problem we wanted to discuss suddenly isn't a problem any more… until it resurfaces again next week. We've done the first part of the work—getting to the dentist or to the meeting—but we haven't carried it through.

The premature celebrations at Heorot when Grendel is dead are just one version of this. There will be another challenge for Beowulf to face; this time, it will be even more demanding than the previous one because it will be out of sight of others entirely. In order to deal with Grendel's mother, the dragon—the root of the curse on Heorot—Beowulf has to descend deep into a lake, deep into his unconscious, and wrestle with the greedy, envious, murderous force that waits there to destroy him. He has to descend to the shadow self and master it fully this time. He has to find it on its home turf, not on his.

For anyone who has felt the emotions of battle and the overwhelming feelings around killing another living being, there is always difficulty in transitioning back to "normal" life. There is a similar struggle for those of us who have fought with mental distress and overcome it—namely, how to live in the everyday world and take it seriously. People who have conquered drug and alcohol addictions face a remarkably similar task: they may have won the battle against the addiction, but they never lose the sense that they could slip back at any time. That's partly why the slogan of Alcoholics Anonymous is "one day at a time," and partly why addicts are always referred to as "in recovery" or "recovering" rather than, say, "cured."

The implications are clear: we can be back in control of ourselves, but the demons are never dead; they still exist. And that's why we have the third monster in this poem.

The final dragon in the story is awakened from its ages-old slumber by a servant who steals a golden cup from its hoard. The servant's greed unleashes the dragon's fury, and Beowulf, who after having reigned well for fifty years must be approaching seventy, puts on his armor and once again gets on with the task of killing the dragon. This time he takes along his retinue. He must know that this adventure is likely to kill him, yet he goes anyway—he has to save his people. If courage is defined by anything, then it has to be defined by the calm determination of the hero to do the task, even though he or she is unlikely to survive.

Beowulf does kill the dragon but, in the process, is badly burned by it. Courageously, he takes on by far the most dangerous task—meeting the dragon head on, while Wiglaf attacks from the side. Beowulf's wounds are so severe that he dies soon afterward. We could say that his example has demonstrated to others an inspirational deed, which will lead everyone to be more courageous in future. We could also say that Beowulf has taught the whole kingdom that courage is as much about working together for a shared outcome as it is about personal glory—both statements would be true. And we could also spell out that our internal demons never go away completely and will be present at our death; in fact, they will help kill us. Courage—real courage—arises because we have looked deep into ourselves, felt the fear, and overcome it.

For Beowulf, this means that he has no option but to act and overcome any natural fear he may feel. He's not going to become suddenly very thoughtful and work out a different way to deal with this creature, one that involves not getting himself killed. He has to be brave because that's the way his psyche has developed, and he dies because of it. He cannot stop being who he is. Like the three tests or riddles that we encounter so often in fairy tales, the three-part structure of the tests that Beowulf experiences serve as a reminder of this deep truth, which we would all do well to recall.

I would like to offer an anecdote or two here to help clarify this point. I am thinking of the old gentleman who had learned early on to be utterly self-reliant, partly as a result of a difficult childhood, then again when his wife died prematurely. He remained doggedly independent until he fell over in his home and died. Had he listened to his family, he might have had any number of safeguards in place, which could have prolonged his days, but he refused them all. The family couldn't quite understand this, but they all agreed it was exactly true to who he was that he should have arranged his life this way, and they greeted his death as being somehow what they would have expected. After being tested on several occasions, he had become self-reliant because it was necessary for his survival, then he continued to live according to that experience. To ask him to stop being so independent would have been like asking him to stop being who he was.

I'm reminded also of my own late father, whose last coherent words were a stream of advice about how to fly different types of aircraft, most of which were by then in museums—if they had survived at all. This was no use whatsoever to my mother, who was the only person present for this conversation; yet, my father was giving her good advice that came from the part of his life when he had been an air force officer flying in those planes, facing death. The trauma that had shaped his life resurfaced in his last hours. This time, he was prepared, but the fight was all internal, and of course, he was beaten in the end.

If *Beowulf* has anything to tell us it would be this message about the nature of our own demons, how to meet them face on, and how, even then, they never really let us go free. The past is never completely over. It is only our wishful thinking as human beings who like closure that leads us to think about killing a dragon as marking the end of anything. Wishful thinking is why the First World War was called "the war to end all wars." Well, it certainly wasn't that, because the peace lasted only twenty years. The Second World War was dubbed as being "the war against fascism," but it would be foolish to claim that fascism ended when the shooting stopped. Fascism is with us now, creeping out of the corners. These evils must be fought every day.

If we can see this pattern we will notice that there are powerful echoes of it in several of Grimm's fairy tales. In "The Golden Bird," for example, we meet three brothers who undergo a test. Then the third and youngest brother, who passes the first test and the second test, finds he has three more tests, followed by three more. It's a long and complex tale, but if we focus on a couple of sections we can perhaps make a parallel with the events we find in *Beowulf*.

At a certain point in "The Golden Bird," the youngest son (there's the youngest son motif again) is advised by a friendly fox to go into a castle, where all the guards are asleep, and to take the golden bird that sits in a plain wooden cage and walk out with it. All will go well, he is told, as long as he doesn't try to put the golden bird in the nearby golden cage. The youngest son finds the bird but feels it would be absurd to leave such a beautiful bird in "a common and ugly cage." Unfortunately, when he attempts to transfer it into the golden cage it wakes up, makes a noise, which in turn wakes the soldiers, and he is captured. His error is not only in not following directions but also in wanting to honor the bird's beauty—a kindly error.

He is condemned to death, unless he can find the golden horse. The fox tells him he should have listened to his advice, but agrees to tell him how to find the golden horse. After a journey to the next castle, he is to walk into the stables, where the horse is kept and where all the grooms are asleep, but he must not put the golden saddle on the horse, just the ordinary wood-and-leather saddle. The young man finds the horse, but feels the "beautiful beast will be shamed" by the common saddle. Again, it's not pride or greed that motivates him but respect for the creature. Of course, the moment he puts the golden saddle on the horse, everyone wakes up and he's captured.

This time, the youngest son can only be spared if he finds the golden maiden. The fox again advises him, shaking its head that the youth didn't follow the instructions fully. Now this situation is exactly the same as before in its general outlines. He must find the castle, wait until the maiden goes to bathe, then he must run up and kiss her. She will immediately offer to follow him, as long as she can say goodbye to her parents first. This he must not allow, says the fox. Well, soft-hearted man that he is, the youngest son does allow it, the whole castle awakens in an uproar, and now he has to move a mountain to escape death. This time it is the fox who moves the mountain. The young man then takes the maiden as his bride, reclaims the horse and the bird, and begins his return home.

The young man's crime, if we could call it that, is being tender-hearted. Then the fox asks for one more thing: the youngest son must shoot him dead and cut off his head and paws. The young man refuses because he says that would scarcely be gratitude to one who had been so helpful to him. It's the exact same fault as before: he won't do as he's told because he has a tender heart. The fox runs off, warning him not to buy any "gallows flesh" and to avoid sitting on the edge of wells. The young man forgets this advice when he buys back his brothers from the gallows, just as they are about to be hanged, and a short time later the rescued brothers almost manage to kill him when he disregards the fox's advice not to sit on the edge of a well. He had forgotten the advice because he was unsuspecting and had a generous heart.

Fortunately, the youngest son is not killed by his fall and appears at his father's castle. When he arrives, the golden bird begins singing again, the golden horse once again eats his fodder, and the golden maiden is delighted. The wicked brothers are punished, and a happy ending seems assured. Years later, the youngest son meets the fox again. This time, he agrees to shoot the fox and cut off its head and paws, thereby releasing the fox from an enchantment—it turns out he's the golden maiden's brother. All three live happily ever after. We might say that the good nature of the young man is now linked to the practical and sly wisdom of the fox, so he will make the right decisions from now on.

In archetypal terms, the youth has to learn to harness his executive power and personal courage to his sense of compassionate understanding. This represents the balance of the Warrior and the Lover archetypes that needs to be worked out before he can become a fully actualized human being.

Clearly, the vision that lies at the heart of this tale is less dark than the one we encounter in *Beowulf*, but it makes a point that is not entirely dissimilar—even virtues can be troublesome, and those character traits never really leave us. Generosity is a virtue, except when it threatens to kill us. Compassion is good, except when murderers are released to kill again. Sometimes we have to do things that we find distasteful.

Other tales offer variations on the three-part structure. It seems to be pretty much universal as an organizing device, and as in *Beowulf*, the three events always build on each other thematically. Three repetitions, after all, establish a pattern. The pattern may have to do with relatively trivial things, or it may have to do with powerful psychic movements. That depends upon the tale.

For our purposes, comparing the Grimm tales with *Beowulf* can lead us in interesting directions. For example, as we've seen in "Little Snow-White," the three temptations are all linked to sexualization. All are aspects of life that Snow-white will have to confront at some point: she will have to pay attention to how she feels about her looks and to her changing body shape (and a corset will change the body's shape, definitely) and she'll have to do this throughout her life. Similarly she will have to face that apple of sexual temptation, too.

These are not issues that go away after being examined once; they tend to come back. Snow-white has learned from them once, it's true; but they'll always be there as challenges, and she'll have to be constantly aware of what is appropriate and when. The stepmother has obviously not managed to learn these lessons, since she's still obsessively interested in remaining the "fairest in the land"—that's what has turned her into a monster. Again, it's our strengths, like the stepmother's beauty and Beowulf's fighting ability, that threaten to turn us into monsters if we don't acknowledge their power and rein them in and use them appropriately.

This pattern repeats often in the tales. Noticing this can tell us how to live, but it's also sobering. To some extent, we are all prisoners of our own character—and our character is the driving force that shapes our lives. We are destined to be true to ourselves, one way or another; it's up to us to decide which self we adopt as the "true" self.

## CHAPTER 13

# "The Glass Coffin"

## Growing Courage

In keeping with the themes of sexuality and the relationship between the sexes, let's now examine "The Glass Coffin" (Tale No. 163), a particularly revealing illustration of the themes. Once again the opening sentence of the tale issues a warning that we're dealing with something unusual:

> Let no one ever say that a poor tailor cannot do great things and
> win high honors; all that is needed is that he should go to the
> right smithy, and what is of most consequence, is that he should
> have good luck.

Why a tailor should go to a blacksmith is not explained, and since blacksmiths aren't mentioned again in the story we could be forgiven for shrugging this off; yet, to ignore any story when it announces its intentions in this way is to ignore the metaphor the story is about to present.

Tailors were legendary for being small, unathletic, and physically unimpressive. Their work required them to bend over their sewing, often sitting cross-legged, and with only their hands moving. Tailors were, therefore, seen as effeminate, or at least not as "real" men; it's a joke that runs through sixteenth- and seventeenth-century drama. So why is this tailor going to a smithy? If we think of a smithy as a place of fire and energy, where metals are made strong and serviceable, we can see that this is a tale about an unpromising young man who gets pounded into shape, like a heated iron implement.

In fact, the tailor starts off every bit as feeble as we might expect. He's lost in a great forest and decides not to sleep on the ground "for fear of wild beasts," so he climbs a tree to spend the night. He tries to sleep "not without fear and trembling," but cannot. That's when he sees a house. He goes to it and finds a little old man, who at first won't let him in. But the tailor pleads and finally gets a bed. The next morning he awakens to the sound of tremendous bellowing and "the tailor, full of unwonted courage" goes outside to see a bull and a stag fighting it out.

The three references to the tailor's courage will not have escaped our notice, especially as the timid tailor who was afraid of wild beasts is now fascinated by the two large creatures before him fighting, until the stag kills the bull. It's as if when he awakens that morning he awakens to a new sense of who he could be.

Before the tailor can think twice, the stag scoops him up on its antlers and runs off with him to a wall of rock, which it pushes with its antlers after having first let the tailor down. A door opens and flames shoot out, which suggests a hell-mouth, or possibly that blacksmith's shop we heard about in the opening sentence. Bemused, the tailor considers running away, but a voice says, "Enter without fear; no evil shall befall you."

A lesser person might still have fled, but the tailor goes in, sees a great stone hall, and hears another voice that says he should step on the stone in the middle of the hall and good fortune will await him. "His courage had already grown so great that he obeyed the order," we are told, and the stone sinks down with him on it into a lower chamber, where he sees a glass case with a miniature castle, glass vases filled with colored liquids or smoke, and a beautiful maiden in a glass coffin.

The maiden awakens, asks him to let her out of the glass coffin, then, we are told, immediately "covered herself with a large cloak." That's when we realize that the maiden who "was wrapped in her long hair as in a precious mantle" was, in fact, otherwise naked. She kisses him on the lips—so we can be in no doubt about the way this story is going—and explains that she will marry him.

Then she tells him the story of the stranger who came to stay with her and her brother. It seemed her brother liked the stranger more than she did, and they enjoyed doing male things like hunting. Then, one night, the stranger came into her bedroom, walking through the two doors that were "fast bolted." He explained that he knew magic, and had "forced his way through all fastenings with the intention of offering his hand and heart." She refused to accept him, and he eventually left.

The next morning she got up, exhausted, to discover that her brother and the stranger had already gone out hunting, the typical male activity of the upper classes at the time. Alarmed by her experiences of the previous evening, she chased after them on horseback and arrived to find her brother had been changed into a stag. The stranger laughed at her; she drew her pistol and shot at him, but the bullet bounced off his breast and killed her horse. When she awoke, she found herself in the glass coffin, with her shrunken castle in the other glass case and all her subjects in the glass vases. The stranger told her that all would be returned to normal if she would comply with his wishes. She remained mute, refusing to give him any answer, and he turned himself into a bull. Imprisoned in the glass coffin, she dreamed that one day a man would come and release her. This bull was the same one the tailor had seen killed only a short time before.

The tailor is evidently the man the princess has awaited, and she is delighted with him. She then asks him for help, and they drag the glass case with the castle in it and the glass vases outside, where the contents miraculously grow to full size and the people pour out and greet each other. When all is returned to normal the maiden marries the tailor, and the stag, which by killing the bull had broken the spell, turns back into her brother.

It's necessary to repeat so much detail here because it's clear that the tale has several themes. One has to do with the tailor's growing courage. He starts off lost and timid, but his courage seems to grow as the story moves forward, although we are told this, rather than shown it at first. When the tailor descends into the depths of the prison, though, I think we can see that he is not short of courage.

The second theme is also fairly clear, and it's about sexual drives. The stag is a noble and very male creature (stags often have harems of many females in the wild) and, as we have seen, it fights and defeats the obvious male energy of the bull. The violent nature and rampant sexuality of the bull would have been obvious to anyone who had ever been near a farm, where bulls are kept for breeding purposes and can be dangerous. By contrast, the more refined delicacy of the stag's physique suggests a wholly different, but equally male, sexual character.

Although today the idea of a "stag party," which many people know better by the name of "bachelor party," has rather dubious associations, it can also be seen as the final celebration of maleness that will be tamed and channeled successfully in marriage. When we add in the fact that the stranger who became the bull is also one who "forces" (as the story tells us) his way into the maiden's bedroom in the middle of the night, we can see that this bull is a creature of sexual predation. He may offer her his hand, but if he were actually an honorable man he'd have done that in broad daylight, presumably with the agreement of her brother. Her refusal to answer him is the only thing possible for her. The stranger's bullish sexual insistence is in direct contrast to the stag's nature.

What this suggests is that the selfish sexual brashness of the stranger is an indication that his behavior is all about having power over others and comes close to rape. When thwarted he imprisons the maiden, which presumably will not get him what he wants, although he says everything will return to the way it was before if she agrees to marry him. She still refuses to speak. He can control her movements and reduce her castle and people to his power, but he cannot control her inner thoughts, her dreams and visions. The glass coffin, therefore, is symbolic of the maiden's attitude, which is "don't touch me"; at the same time, it is also a symbol of the possessive sexuality of the stranger, whose actions convey: "If I can't have her, then no one else can." This sort of double-sided symbol is particularly effective in conveying a complex meaning in a compressed form.

When we consider the other versions of masculinity this tale gives us, the tailor, who is not really in the same class of dominating maleness as the stranger, is to some extent the perfect mate for the princess. He sets her free, he gives her back what's hers, and he isn't going to force anyone to do anything. In this way he is more respectful, and certainly gentler; moreover, he's not without courage, so he's not contemptible. One might say that the "smithy" he visits, as the opening sentence alerts us, is the process that allows him to grow in courage and in worth. He's refined and strengthened, like a piece of iron that is worked by a blacksmith until it becomes a piece of steel. He had these qualities all along. He simply never had the opportunity to use them before.

The tale offers a basic truth for us today—that a beautiful woman surrounded by alpha males may, in fact, be repelled by their overly macho behavior and retreat into her own glass coffin, refusing their advances and becoming more and more remote. The maiden's womanly nature has indeed gone underground. What brings her back to life and to the open air is the gentleness of the tailor, and when she emerges everything is ready to reassume its true dimensions; she is ready to share her riches with the world again.

We can see this again and again around us, if we look. Beautiful women do not always gravitate toward the dominant males of our society; instead, they may choose a gentler mate. For instance, the late Peter Sellers was a wonderful comedian but hardly a ferocious male presence—and certainly not on screen—but he was always seen with the most beautiful women of the time, and over the years he was married to four of them. Perhaps it was his ability to make women laugh that melted their hearts. Whatever his secret, he won these beautiful women by not being the stereotypical hunk. One could add Jim Carrey and former Playboy Bunny Jenny McCarthy as examples, although neither is lacking in physical charm. In an interview conducted when Carrey was on a charity walk with McCarthy's autistic son, he explained that people only saw him as a comedian, but that didn't mean he didn't have other qualities. Another example might be the unathletic Woody Allen, who seems to have no trouble at all charming the beautiful women in his life.

In terms of sexual behaviors, the man who acts like a bull in the bedroom may find that at some point he is frozen out of the relationship, since most women, quite naturally, want some intimacy and understanding and not just unbridled sex all the time. A strong sex drive is never enough on its own for a successful marriage.

The killing of the bull by the stag represents the moderation of the sexuality required in a reasonable loving relationship, and the ultimate transformation of the stag back into the human form of the brother suggests that the brother has a sense of this lesson, too. He's enjoyed his time hunting with his macho friend, but he knows the limits of that sort of relationship. Significantly, he doesn't object in any way to the tailor, who has no money and no status. He accepts that this may be just the husband his sister needs after her difficult experience.

Behind this may be an echo of the popular legends about the unicorn. In mythology, the unicorn was a ferocious fighter; he could be tamed and captured only by a virgin before whom he became totally acquiescent. It seems as if this stag has some of the properties of the mythic beast, since he guards his virgin sister; when seen in this way, the tale is certainly a depiction of different sexual behaviors, so the echo has some significance.

There is also a more readily available meaning for us: the stag grows its horns and sheds them each year. Each year, the new horns become larger with more points, and the stag will use them for display, to overawe rivals for mates, and to fight if need be. We realize that, until now, the stag in the tale has been unable to fight the bull. His horns have been neither big enough nor strong enough.

This detail, which would have been fairly clear to European village dwellers when the story was recorded, lets us know that this is a tale about time and timing. There is a moment when actions become possible. The stag seizes the moment when he is ready to face the bull, and in his own way the tailor does, too. He accepts what chance has thrown in his way, and he, too, grows in stature to meet his good fortune. The stranger who becomes the bull pushes his sexual claims on the sister in a way that is neither appropriate nor timely. Moreover, if we take the attempted rape theme a little farther, we can say that this whole tale is certainly an insightful description of what can happen to young women who have been frightened by this type of experience. They may well feel helpless and retreat into themselves.

The silence the maiden offers as her only response to the stranger is mirrored to some extent by the reluctance of clients in therapeutic settings to talk about such issues. It is often extremely difficult to get women to talk about their experiences of being sexually assaulted, for example. When the woman finally feels safe enough to talk, though, she will feel a sense of relief in telling her entire life story to those she feels she can trust.

And that's exactly what the maiden does. She refuses even to talk to the stranger, but she tells the tailor everything. We must remember here that she was asleep in her glass coffin. She knows she's been seen in her nakedness, covered only by her very long golden hair, and that this suggests the experience of being seen, free of disguises or evasions, without being embarrassed or humiliated. In fact, it is a delicate metaphor for the condition of being understood and accepted without being judged. In addition, this time she knows that the situation is different from what happened in the bedroom, when she was awakened in a very different way.

It's schematic, but it is a description that corresponds closely to what I've observed when working with clients who have been sexually assaulted. Once they feel they've been accepted, without being criticized, they can for the first time spill out their hearts about the event that they have kept quiet about for all those years. In many ways, the tale conveys an insight that can help us recognize those who have been victimized, then see what they need in order to heal.

Another significant feature of this tale, as we've seen in many others that share aspects of its plot and design, is the descent into the Underworld. In classical Greek mythology, descending into the Underworld, or Hades, meant visiting the dead. To some extent the maiden *is* dead—all her beauty and wealth are locked away, and she's effectively dead to the world, totally inaccessible.

Bringing the dead back from Hades was a task that required courage and absolute faith. Orpheus loses Eurydice, as we may recall, because he looks back to make sure she's following, and he's been forbidden to look back.[1] The tailor has no such doubts or fears; he just does what seems necessary. When the maiden tells him she'll marry him, he doesn't hesitate. He doesn't ask her if she means it or how they'll live on his pay, even though she promises to marry him before the castle has been returned to its proper dimensions. He simply accepts.

So what does this tell us? In some ways, this is a splendidly democratic tale since it suggests that anyone, even a poor tailor, can grow spiritually, if he is fortunate enough to go through some hardships. Tailors would usually be found in towns, working indoors, but this tailor has had the courage to go out into the world, as a Pilgrim, and he's got himself lost. In getting lost, he has also lost his old way of being, his tailor's timidity. He witnesses the deep passions of nature in the bull and the stag, then allows himself to explore the inner nature of his own psyche, the descent into the unconscious.

What he discovers there are the suppressed longings of his dreams. The beautiful woman who will love him, the castle—these are aspects of a fantasy life that most males have but which are very often repressed and condemned to remain in the unconscious. We think the beautiful future can never happen to us. We give up on our dreams, and our souls are the poorer for it. Freed from his usual experience of life and work, the tailor finds inside himself the wealth contained in his longings; with their guidance, he brings this wealth to the surface, where it becomes real. We can all do this, if we listen to what is deep within us and follow its guidance. Mostly, though, we are too frightened to do this.

It is fear of what we may find that stops us uncovering our own internal riches. When the tailor meets the maiden, he is meeting not just his repressed longings but also those feminine aspects of himself that, as a male, he will have repressed—his anima. His task can be seen as the Warrior archetype finding the Lover archetype, the male animus finding the female anima and bringing them together. He will marry the maiden and produce children. The meaning is clear: if we don't find within our deep souls the opposite of ourselves, we cannot become fully productive, nor can we be fully and completely ourselves. This is the journey of the psyche, the pilgrimage to completeness that we are invited to make, and which many people turn down.

In the everyday world, the fearful "tailors" might be those of us who say we will, one day, take up art, or music, or poetry, or playwriting, or follow our dream again; for now, though, we don't have time or we feel we can't quit our day job. Occasionally, chance flings us an opportunity. It may happen, for example, when we lose a job and start to do creative things during this time of enforced waiting, only to find that the creative activity is far more compelling than anything else. When we honor this part of ourselves, the suppressed part, we are meeting the creative "opposite" of who we usually find ourselves forced to be. This is the free part of our psyche that has been waiting for long years to come back into the light again, just as the princess has. At first sight it may seem totally impractical and impossible—the princess must at first seem like a lunatic to the tailor—but we have to learn from the tailor to accept what comes to us in this way, for it is the way forward that our souls need.

The old joke is that every waiter in New York City is an actor waiting for a break. I've never understood why that would be anything but a cause for celebration. Think of it: all those people who really want to explore acting and theater and who are willing to put a conventional career on hold to do it. It's inspiring! Some, obviously, are thinking only of money and fame, but it's still better than giving up hope and knuckling down to some soul-deadening routine just to get a paycheck. The tale is clear about this: when we go into that deep interior space of dreams and longings, whether we choose to go there or circumstances throw us there, we can become an entirely different person. But it takes courage.

Many of us remain stuck in our lives because we just can't imagine anything else, anything better. Just thinking this way creates a self-fulfilling prophecy, and sure enough, we don't get anything else. The tailor, up his tree, could have stayed there, but he goes to the house, asks for shelter, and when it's refused, remains insistent about what he wants until he gets it. Even at this basic level, the tailor doesn't settle for second best.

I think of the tailor, sometimes, when I'm in a café or a restaurant and perhaps the waiter brings me something that isn't quite right. Just to avoid a fuss, I might smile and say, "That's alright," and accept what I'm given. It's a small compromise—I'm not suggesting we should all become difficult when we're in restaurants—but also a symptom of what we may do in the rest of our lives, if we don't pay attention to our thinking. For in the larger aspects of life, if we go into our psyches and allow ourselves to acknowledge our yearnings, we can then mobilize the energy to find what we want and bring those longings into the light of day.

It's hard to overstate the importance of this symbol of the descent into the self, into the unconscious, if only because it occurs in so many of the tales. The word "unconscious," used in the way we're using it here, did not come into common usage until a century after the Grimm brothers published the tales, but it is clear that folk wisdom has always known about the power of the deep psyche, since the tales render it in such convincing ways. There's never any doubt that looking deep inside oneself is something that has value.

Before leaving this tale there is one other aspect of behavior to examine—an aspect that is the exact opposite of the productive descent into the self we've just seen: it hinges on the figure of the stag. The meaning of the stag is hard to reconstruct with any accuracy since there are so many legends and meanings attached to stags.[2] We can be sure of only a few things. One is that the stag is a noble animal that is revered and accorded status almost universally; another is that stags are hunted and killed primarily as trophies, since their meat is less tasty than the venison of the doe.

In turning the young prince into a stag, the stranger is both acknowledging the prince's finer nature and putting him into a very vulnerable situation, by turning him into quarry that anyone could easily hunt down and destroy. With these actions, we gain a fascinating psychological insight into the mind of a sexual manipulator. He may make a play for the sister of his friend, using his status with the brother to try and coerce sexual favors, while at the same time dominating and enjoying the power he has over the brother, making a fool of him in a sadistic fashion. Psychologically speaking, this is the classic "splitting" technique. It usually depends upon each person, or group of people, being fed a slightly different version of what is going on. The most obvious version of this is a child who tells Mom that Dad has said something is a good idea, then informs Dad that Mom has said it's a good idea.

There is an exceptionally fine example of this "splitting technique" in award-winning journalist Lynn Barber's memoir of her teenage years in the 1960s, *An Education*, excerpts of which appeared in the British Sunday newspaper *The Observer*, and which has been turned into a movie.[3]

In the memoir, Ms. Barber describes how her older admirer Simon succeeded in inveigling his way into her bed by simultaneously being nice to her and "wooing" her conservative parents, so that the parents let down their guard, leaving their daughter almost defenseless. This parental approval was eventually so strong that she felt she couldn't refuse Simon's plans for her, even though she was a gifted student with a place at Oxford University awaiting her, didn't really love Simon, and knew that becoming his wife would prevent her from going to college at all. This must have been hard enough, but Simon turned out to be already married: his manipulation was a power play to satisfy his own desires and to make fools of both parents and daughter.

To some extent, this is what we see in this tale—the stranger who seems fond of the brother and is using it as a way to ensnare the sister and, ultimately, humiliate them both. It's ugly stuff but only too recognizable. It's exactly the sort of behavior we can expect from someone who sees only what he *thinks* he wants—someone who has never made that deep descent into the self that allows him to become sufficiently aware of what he *needs*. It's a shortcut based on deception. Those who deceive others are basically deceiving themselves as to the real value of what will result.

## CHAPTER 14

# "Little Briar-Rose"

## Family Birth Order;
## Sleep As Metaphor

So far, in discussing the Grimm brothers' fairy tales and folktales, we've noticed several tendencies: for events to happen in threes, with the last event having more significance than the previous two, and preference shown by a parent toward the youngest brother or sister, or the "simple" character. These tendencies often get combined in the idea of three brothers or three sisters, the youngest of whom is usually braver, kinder, more insightful, or in some way better than the others. This is the character who very often solves the problem of the tale, as is the case in "The Crystal Ball" (Tale No. 197), "The Sea Hare" (Tale No. 191), "The Hut in the Forest" (Tale No. 169), "Cinderella," and other tales.

The wisdom here is something that comes straight out of the direct observation of family dynamics and is often noticeable when there are several children in a family. Put simply: the third child faces a different struggle within the family structure compared with the other two siblings.

Typically, a firstborn receives a lot of parental attention right from the start. This may lead the child to follow the parents' dictates and conform, or if the parents are too strict, run away. The parental pressure is clear in "Little Snow-White," for example, where it takes the form of jealousy. In "Little Briar-Rose" (Tale No. 50), it veers to the opposite extreme, taking the shape of overprotectiveness. In that tale, which most of us know by the Disney title of "Sleeping Beauty," the king orders the destruction of all spindles in the kingdom to prevent his daughter ever being harmed by one. This sounds sensible, until we realize that, in early times, the spinning of thread and making of clothes was almost as vital work for women as ploughing and tilling the fields was for men. The king's overprotectiveness of his firstborn, therefore, goes against the common good.

A secondborn may be rebellious, too, but this child's struggle is to get equal recognition from the family as a whole since, at this point, the family will be pretty busy meeting their daily needs, and the extra child can claim less from them. The tales are often very vague about the secondborn. We have plenty of sets of twins—"The Two Brothers" (Tale No. 60), "The Gold Children" (Tale No. 85), and others—and we have the strange but almost twinlike situation of "Hänsel and Gretel," where we do not know which sibling is older. The same seems to be true of "Brother and Sister," as we saw in Chapter 3. In that tale, the brother is the impulsive sibling, who has to be looked after by his sister, which suggests he's younger; yet, he refers to her as "my little sister."

The predicament of the secondborn, therefore, does not seem to register in these tales. The single exception seems to be in "One-Eye, Two-Eyes, and Three-Eyes" (Tale No.130). There, the firstborn sister has one eye, the secondborn sister has two eyes, and the thirdborn sister has three eyes. The firstborn and thirdborn think they're special (which they are, although not in the way they think). They despise their more normal sister with two eyes, but she turns out to be far more acceptable to the knight who arrives and carries her away. It's her humility and her generosity that makes Two-Eyes desirable, as well as her beauty, which the other sisters refuse to acknowledge. The situation of the middle child seems rather deftly depicted, right there.

The thirdborn, the "youngest" in some tales, tends to get treated in yet another way. This child may become a spoiled favorite, like the princess in "The Frog-King," or a bit of a loner, outside the main dramas of the home, and, therefore, more thoughtful, even more tender-hearted. This can be viewed as "simpleminded," or as loving. If we think about this for a moment, it makes sense that the thirdborn should be more sensitive to the claims of others, and more polite than the older siblings. Within the family structure the thirdborn is very likely to be less capable because he or she is younger; thus, getting treated well during childhood may depend upon being nice, being accepted, and being just a little more alert to nuances of behavior than the other siblings. This has the ring of truth. The weaker figures in the world really do have to pay closer attention to what's going on. The powerful never have to rethink how they live. Why should they? They're powerful and successful. It's the less successful people who have to think, observe, and innovate. For many people, it is only a reversal of fortune or a defeat that causes them to reconsider what they do and how they do it.

In this way the tales revalue the power of thinking, of adapting, and of personal growth by showing us the thirdborn child finding solutions undreamed-of by the other siblings. In "The Sea Hare," the thirdborn son sees his older siblings fail to win the princess and have their heads cut off for their trouble. As a charming third son, though, we can assume that he is used to manipulating a situation within the family where he has no power, as he is the one who succeeds in talking his way into a better arrangement. He's able to persuade the princess to give him not just one try to win her (as his brothers had) but three. Now, that's a smooth operator.

The tale goes on to tell us that the task for this youngest son is to avoid being seen by the princess from her tower, which, with its extraordinary windows, allows her to see inside everything. So the youngest son has himself transformed into a "Sea Hare," who is so cuddly the unwitting princess buys him the day before. When she goes to her special watchtower to look for him, the Sea Hare climbs into her braids, snuggling like a kitten, but cannot be seen by the princess because he's right under her chin. Talk about someone who gets in under the radar! It's the sort of trickster behavior we can expect from a thirdborn. It also tells us some good home truths about how people tend to function in the world—the powerful look outward but not at what's under their noses.

Obviously, this sort of stereotype is not true of every family; however, I think we can see that the tales are reflecting what is a general and recognizable tendency, so that the listeners or readers would be able to say, yes, that can indeed be true of the thirdborn. In my Swiss grandfather's family, for example, it was expected that the first son would inherit the farm, the second would be a teacher, and the third would go into law, where the thirdborn's persuasive ability could be used to good effect. This pattern had existed in that rural corner of Switzerland for a very long time.

Today we have sociologists with surveys who pretty much confirm what had been known as "folk wisdom" for generations. Frank Sulloway's careful study of birth order *Born to Rebel* addresses the topic in exactly this way, and comes to approximately the same conclusions.[1] For our purposes, though, what we need to register is that the tales reward and praise the ability to think differently (an innovative idea) but insist that the protagonist should behave well (a conservative idea). The tales, therefore, show us how to work within the existing social structure, rather than how to destroy or change it.

Another feature of the tales that we encounter frequently is the situation in which the characters fall asleep, or are enchanted, or are even locked away for many years.

This is most obvious in "Little Briar-Rose," where Briar-rose is pricked by the spindle and the whole kingdom goes into a deep sleep for two hundred years before the prince's kiss awakens her. Since she's fifteen when she is pricked by the spindle—and spinning was often the main activity of unmarried women who were waiting for a mate—it suggests that her "sleep" is a metaphor for the sort of dreamy cluelessness some girls drift around in when they're going through puberty and adolescence.

At this age, some young women seem to go into their own private world. They either enter an introverted world of reading, reserve, and personal absorption in an activity (such as sports, or writing poetry, or collecting things), or go into an extroverted world of activity that seems self-centered. In each case, it's a world that is out of touch with daily reality, as the parents perceive it. Exasperating as this may be for parents, it would be a mistake to say that nothing is going on during this time—it just is difficult to describe! When Briar-rose is awakened by the prince, it is because the briars that have protected her all this time now open a path for him because the time is now right.

These periods of withdrawing and going into a kind of "sleep," therefore, signal to us that something is changing—something that should not be disturbed. Anyone who has gone to bed exhausted and awakened feeling refreshed knows this, and it's the genius of the tales that they use this most familiar of experiences as part of what they need to convey at a deep level. Change happens, it has to be accommodated, and it cannot be rushed. One might say that when girls are ready for romance and to select a life partner they become ready in their own time, because this is an internal process that has very little to do with peer pressure. Until then, they may look the same as before, but those thorn bushes won't let anyone close. This is, to some extent, what we see in the symbolism of the church wedding. The groom waits at the altar, and the bride arrives in her own time, signaling that this is now a voluntary giving of herself.

That sounds pretty basic. If only more of today's parents understood it. A staggering number go to considerable expense to place their children in special learning programs and buy educational software to promote learning (much of which doesn't seem to work). They push their children into accelerated programs of one sort or another, leaving the child no time to be alone. The makers of these "educational" toys are making plenty of money, of course, feeding parents' neuroses about how their children will fare in the adult world. But the over-scheduled child—the child who has no quiet time alone to think things through at her own pace—is a child who feels confused later on. That's because few of the internal mechanisms for motivation are permitted to establish themselves when a child is overscheduled and pushed. This may be part of the reason we have so many young people today who don't seem to care very much about anything, and who believe in very little aside from their own comfort and gain.

When I worked with disturbed adolescents in England, in a residential community setting, an accepted axiom of treatment was that these very damaged young people would be drifting around doing nothing very much for about two years. Then, gradually, they would begin to want to take classes and take charge of their lives. This two-year period was hardly "sleep" because plenty of behavioral issues came up; yet, it was a time in which the young people were permitted to drift, so that they could come to a new understanding of themselves.

Some of the funding authorities who paid the fees for teens to attend the group home understood this; others did not. They wanted a visible return on their investment within days. Government departments run by people who were supposed to be specialists in the field sometimes displayed the most alarming lack of awareness about what was going on. The period of dormancy these adolescents needed so they could rethink, reassess, and relearn behaviors, well, these required more time than the spreadsheets would allow. Young lives were ruined because of this short-sightedness. The tales we've been examining seem far more attuned to what psychic healing may be about. It's part of their deep wisdom. We need these tales more than ever, for the ways they spell out problems that beset us every day, and for the ways they lead us to an awareness of what it takes to heal those situations.

Grimm's fairy tales are not the answer to all the world's ills; however, in this book, I have tried to show that they are tales that have considerable insight and wisdom for us if we are prepared to look for it. They cover many of life's more troublesome and difficult-to-discuss aspects, from sexual jealousy and the effects of rape and incest to issues that have to do with the emerging of sexual identity. Incest and rape don't have to have actually occurred for tensions around these issues to exist and be felt by the child or young person or adult. The tales have an unerring courage in naming the situations, and, most importantly, they also show us the way out of the particular problem.

These tales take the ordinary tensions that inevitably exist in any family grouping or small community and write them large so we can consider them. Exaggeration and storytelling have their uses. They allow us to talk about something without feeling it is about us personally. Talking about the predatory sexuality of the stranger in "The Glass Coffin," for example, does not expose or embarrass the person who has seen such manipulations in action. This allows for understanding, for added distance, and for healing. In one important aspect, though, the tales do not exaggerate—in the way they handle the deep journey of the soul toward integration with its repressed aspects, what that looks like and requires of us, and above all, why it is necessary. The triumph of these Grimm tales is that they approach these difficult topics with memorable and haunting stories, so that we can reflect on them in our own way and in our own time. They make the issues less abstract and more manageable. That is their real genius.

# Afterword

## Why These Particular Tales?

In this book I've focused on several fairy tales in the Grimm brothers' collection that may be unfamiliar to some readers. There are two reasons for this:

First, I do not wish to repeat material others have written about "Little Red-Cap" ("Little Red Riding Hood," in popular parlance), or spend a lot of time on "Little Snow-White" ("Snow White and the Seven Dwarfs" in Disney's construction), or on other tales that seem to have been treated with respect by other intelligent writers. I decided to include "The Frog-King" and "Cinderella" because I feel that they have been badly mauled by our culture and deserve a fresh look.

Second, the most popular tales are frequently found among the first fifty or sixty tales in the Grimm brothers' collection—it is almost as if readers manage to get about a quarter of the way into the book, then stop. This may be because many of the first tales in the book are more accessible to children, can be understood by children, and do not contain too much overt sexual material—at least, at first sight—so they receive the most exposure as bedtime stories. Children love repetition in stories. It's likely, then, that old favorites are the ones that have become more and more familiar while others have been ignored. Like a favorite toy, some tales get worn to shreds, while others are left almost unused.

Sadly, this means a lot of excellent stories are neglected—tales that may have been ignored because they are puzzling or because they ask us to stretch our awareness as adults. For we may want to remind ourselves that these stories were not just for children but for adults, too, at least originally. Of course, if we're looking only to entertain children, some tales will be bypassed.

Another reason stories are neglected has to do with association: a demanding tale in the collection may be grouped with several others that are second rate, or with tales that are basically jokes, which may lead to it being bypassed. After all, there are more than two hundred tales in the Grimm collection, so readers may well skip over those tales they feel are too demanding. This is how wisdom gets lost.

What is most important to remember is that the tales we have looked at are just some of those that can provide significant psychological insights. They describe particular points of crisis any individual might face, and they also offer a way to understand and solve these crises. The wisdom they have for us, therefore, is of a specific kind. It is the wisdom of psychic healing. That is the sort of wisdom that should on no account be lost.

## Thematic Learning

Part of the reason present day readers tend not to pay close attention to these tales is, as we've seen, that there is a fair amount of thematic duplication and repetition. Repetitions like this are the opposite of what we've come to expect from our modern works of art. This is only because we are so familiar with our own culture's repetitive forms that we overlook them. We regard them as normal; consequently, unfamiliar forms from bygone eras may cause us to misunderstand what we are looking at.

These tales depend upon repetition. They were certainly repeated around the fireside, at gatherings that included several stories each time. One ghost story builds on another, as we know, in approximately the same way, and each gains power from the one that went before. Grimm's tales echo each other and would have been greeted with delight for precisely that reason. This process would have allowed the symbolic elements to be more easily identified.

This is a different way of "knowing" than is usual for us today, perhaps, but it is important because it draws attention to the symbolic structures contained within the tales. So, as we've already seen, the mere mention of the thirdborn child or Simpleton would have had immediate associations for the audience at the time, built up through many tales. These are meanings that may not be easily understood today. What we have is a symbolic shorthand that would have been available to the readers and listeners at the time.

Hollywood still works in the same way, broadly speaking. Watch almost any mainstream Hollywood movie today and you can tell who is going to fall in love with whom within ten minutes of the start of the movie. As with fairy tales, in a movie the reasons for the attraction are telegraphed to us in ways that are not "realistic" but which may be convincing enough for the ninety minutes the audience will be sitting in the theater. Princesses and kings are in short supply these days, but with their physical good looks, beautiful actresses and actors signal the same message of desirability contained in the old tales. Meanwhile, the less attractive people in the cast are more likely to be bad guys or witches and wizards.

In today's movies the storytelling methods are the same, generally, as the formulae we see in fairy tales; it's just that the messages movies convey are often so feeble. Hollywood seems reluctant to show characters undergoing real, deep change: we have all the machinery in place, but the movies sometimes do not deliver anything worthwhile in terms of insights into human psychology. As with the tale of "The Three Spinners," Hollywood tales are frequently unsatisfactory because the plot problem gets solved without any meaningful learning on the part of the main characters—the plot is reduced to the level of a puzzle in which it is the "how" of the plot resolution that matters more than the "why."

The best of Grimms' tales always cause us to ask "why?" Why does the hero of "The Golden Bird" keep making those mistakes? Why does the Skillful Huntsman act in the way he does? Why does Snow-white's stepmother hate her so rabidly? When we ask "why," we move into the realm of psychology.

The insights offered by these tales can smooth many difficult life passages, if we pay attention to them. That is why the very finest of these tales are, first and foremost, healing tales. They describe, in detail, difficult and painful situations, then use this understanding to show us a way forward.

We can, if we choose, place the tales we've looked at in four groups:

- **Tales that focus on the universal issue of personal and sexual maturation** ("The Frog-King," "Cinderella," "Little Briar-Rose," and "Faithful John"): In these tales, the individuals concerned have to learn something about themselves, so that they can develop loving relationships, a lesson with universal applications for all of us.

- **Tales that focus on surviving a specific assault to the self** ("Little Snow-White," "Allerleirauh," and "Hans the Hedgehog"): These tales are concerned with a family rift, in which either parents reject children or children reject parents, one of the most difficult crises anyone could face. The situation may resonate with only a few readers, but it will be familiar in its general outlines to everyone, since we all have to define where we stand in relationship to our parents at some point.

- **Tales concerned with particular life passages** ("Brother and Sister"): This tale focuses on postpartum depression, where the struggle is internal. The emphasis in the tale is on understanding a situation, so that it can be resolved, and respecting the internal processes involved.

- **Tales that allow the characters to descend into the realm of the uncon-**

**scious, where they meet the shadow self and learn to accept what it has to show them** ("The Glass Coffin," "The Three Feathers," "The Skillful Huntsman," and "The Robber Bridegroom"):

This is a journey that will cause the reader to think about his or her core self, so it represents the most demanding and most fully expressed of the psychic material. "The Glass Coffin" and "The Skillful Huntsman" may be the most interesting of this group, since both the hero and heroine make a descent into the unconscious. The young huntsman makes a journey to the center of his being. When he gets there, he finds and observes the princess, who is witnessed from the outside, doing the same thing. It lets us know that we can undertake an internal journey either as part of a physical pilgrimage, or in a quieter, more introverted way. Both methods represent important spiritual events that lead to the soul of the Pilgrim becoming whole.

## Beyond Categorization

The problem with separating out the tales into the above categories, useful though they may be, is that it is simplistic; a careful examination of the tales will show us that they have a way of spanning several categories. The tale of "Cinderella" is certainly about maturation, but Cinderella herself, in her time spent in the ashes, has clearly made some sort of descent into the deep knowledge of who she is. So, perhaps, we might simply say that the *emphasis* in "Cinderella" is more upon maturation than upon the descent into the self.

My aim is not to shove these tales into convenient boxes—it can't really be done. Rather, my intention is to show that there are very different emphases at work. It's not that one tale is better or worse than another but that they're moving in slightly different directions, exploring the richness and variety of the human experience, and inevitably, some go deeper than others.

The great mythologist Joseph Campbell can be of help here, by summing up what is already implicit in the tales—that the descent into the self can be accomplished in a variety of ways.

> When you have found the center within yourself that is the counterpoint of the sacred space, you do not have to go into the forest.... You can live from that center, even while you remain in relation to the world.[1]

In other words, the deep soul work we have seen the male characters achieve by going into the forest can be done in a different way, usually by the female characters, without ever leaving home. This is what Cinderella does in the ashes, and almost all the female characters we've met do it, too. The princess in "Allerleirauh" goes into the forest *and* into the kitchen's ashes, as if to assure us that this is the same journey.

In each case the Grimm brothers' tales describe a situation, then offer us a way forward, so that we can process these events in a way that leads to personal growth and empowerment: they are truly tales that promote a return to wholeness. This is important because people living in the countryside in the eighteenth and nineteenth centuries or earlier really only had folktales or the Bible for guidance.

For centuries the Bible was the single most important literary force, but, unfortunately, it was Holy Writ—it told people how to live but not what the process of living felt like. It was spiritual guidance, not a series of insights into how to handle personal conflicts. Jesus's life might have been a good thing to emulate, but those who did tended to become priests or hermits. Reading about Jesus can give us many insights into many things, but it doesn't offer us much guidance about choosing a mate or what that process will feel like.

Folktales, however, were widely circulated. They may have been in wide circulation even before the Bible reached Europe, and many were valued as practical guides to the problems of everyday living. If the Bible really had satisfied all the needs of the populace, then the tales would have died out before the medieval period. Instead, they endured. More children today know about Snow-white than about the Sermon on the Mount, which, like it or not, tells us something about the way these tales capture our imaginations. In these pages we have looked at some, but certainly not all, of these tales of healing, growth, and empowerment. There are plenty more for the attentive reader.

# The Historical Context

### Sex, Fairy tales, and the
### Romantic Movement

In this book I make a number of statements about the way sex and unconscious urges of various sorts can be viewed in fairy tales. At first sight this may seem unlikely because we tend to think of the storytellers the Grimm brothers used as sources as being rustic German peasants who kept sex in the bedroom and knew nothing of the unconscious.

Nothing could be farther from the truth. The period in which the Grimm brothers launched their books was one in which the primary motivations of human beings were thought to be more fully expressed and more fully felt in folktales and fairy tales than practically anywhere else.

First published in 1812, the Grimm brothers' fairy tale collection was a virtual overnight sensation. Its success was due in part to the influence of the Romantic movement, which began toward the end of the eighteenth century and was in full force in the early 1800s. The Romantics revered the primacy of personal emotional experience. That often meant they regarded rustic and peasant experiences as, in some ways, more "pure" than other experiences because they were closer to nature. Germany was, some might argue, the true center of the Romantic movement, with Schiller, Goethe, Novalis, and Kleist as its poetic voices, although it was a Europe-wide phenomenon. So the Grimm brothers were publishing for a readership that was already eager for what they had to offer.

This preference for songs and poems about rustic life was more than just a local phenomenon. In Great Britain, for example, William Wordsworth, that country's most impressive Romantic poet, revered the songs of fieldworkers and the lives of the ordinary and very poor. *Lyrical Ballads* (1798), a collection of poems that Wordsworth and fellow poet Samuel Coleridge compiled specifically to explore the insights of the rustic experience, was written in "the ordinary language of men," a move that was considered revolutionary at the time. Wordsworth went on to base his entire poetic career on the Preface he wrote for *Lyrical Ballads*. *The Ruined Cottage* soon followed. *The Prelude*, a poem that eventually grew to thirteen books, which Wordsworth worked on until his death, was published in different versions in 1799, 1805, and 1850. Meanwhile, Coleridge's experiments with opium and creativity later placed him in the camp of those who believed in allowing the unconscious to come to the surface in poetic expression (the epic poem "Kubla Khan" was famously conceived in an opium dream).

In addition, the extraordinary success of Robert Burns (1759–1796), the Scottish "ploughman poet," would perhaps not have been possible a hundred years earlier, when there was no taste for his style of dialect writing, which was felt to be truer to authentic human nature than the more refined writing of earlier authors.

In the United States, the effect of this movement was felt in the same way and can be traced even to the Declaration of Independence, which famously stated that "all men are created equal"—an assertion that would have been heaped with scorn even fifty years earlier. The sense of individual experience as valid allowed Henry Wadsworth Longfellow to receive popular acclaim for his book *Hiawatha* (1855), a retelling of American Indian stories for an eager public. All these writers, and their readers, were fascinated by the insights they felt were available only in such authentic folk writings.

This is the background against which the Grimm brothers' tales need to be assessed. In fact, the brothers vacillated about whether to produce some of the tales in their original dialect forms because, as they noted, even though High German added clarity of understanding, it also "lost in flavor, and no longer had such a firm hold of the kernel of the thing signified."[1]

Additional context for the tales is reflected in the comments of philosopher Arthur Schopenhauer, who, in 1819, made use of the concept of the unconscious and acknowledged the strength of the sexual urge that was often expressed in this way: "Man is incarnate sexual instinct, since he owes his origin to copulation, and the wish of his wishes is to copulate."[2] This was almost eighty years before Sigmund Freud became a recognized name in his assessments of the sexual content of literature, specifically in his writings about Oedipus. All of this serves to show that the world that first read the Grimm brothers' tales was already attuned to a sense of the deep and powerful currents available in folk culture, and would not have been unaware of discussions of sexual themes or imagery.

Grimms' Fairy Tales may have been relegated to the nursery in more recent times, but when they were first published, these were not seen as minor tales only suitable for children. They were felt to contain important insights into human nature, flashes of real wisdom that were hard to express any other way. This wisdom is, as always, knowledge that can help us heal.

## Introduction

1. The Jewish Teaching Story is from Annette Simmons, *The Story Factor: Inspiration, Influence, and Persuasion Through the Art of Storytelling* (Cambridge, MA: Perseus, 2002), p. 27. This is a wonderful book about the power of story.

2. "The Man Panel" discussions were organized by Laura Warrell, in Boston, Massachusetts, in 2009. They remain very successful.

3. The fairy godmother appears in Charles Perrault's version, *Histoires ou Contes du Temps passé*, (1697). This is widely available in English under the title *Mother Goose Tales*. There are literally hundred of variants, some ancient but mostly modern, of the tale of Cinderella.

4. Walt Disney Pictures' *The Princess and the Frog* (2009) is set in New Orleans, and the princess of the title is not a princess at all. Disney has produced a long series of such altered fairy tales. In 1937, "Little Snow-White" was transformed into *Snow White and the Seven Dwarfs*; in 1950, *Cinderella* appeared with the fairy godmother and pumpkin included; in 1959, "Little Briar-Rose" became *Sleeping Beauty*; 1989 saw the appearance of *The Little Mermaid,* which derives from Hans Christian Anderson's story; in 1991, *Beauty and the Beast* (which is not a Grimm tale) was released; and 1992 saw the appearance of *Aladdin.* The Disney rewriting of familiar stories is extensive. The studio has announced that for Christmas 2010 *Rapunzel* will be released, the 49th such Disney Animated Classic. Under these circumstances, it is not merely nitpicking to challenge the marketing of such stories that have been designed to maximize the cross-merchandizing of princess dolls of various sorts.

5. Bruno Bettelheim, *The Uses of Enchantment* (New York: Vintage, 1977*)*.

6. Robert Bly, *Iron John* (Boston: Addison-Wesley, 1990).

7. The story of Echo and Narcissus is found in Ovid's *Metamorphoses*, Book III.

8. All quotations from the Grimm brothers' tales are from *The Complete Grimm's Fairy Tales*, intro. Padraic Colum, (New York: Pantheon,1944). Revised and corrected text by James Stern, (New York: Random House, 1972).

9. Frau Viehmann. Joseph Campbell gives a detailed historical assessment of the

way the Grimm brothers used their source material. In *Grimm's Fairy Tales* op. cit., pp. 833–856.

10. "The time of Luther". The comment is found in *Grimm*, op. cit. pp. 833–834.

11. Ruth Bottigheimer, *Fairy Tales: A New History* (New York: State University of New York Press, 2009).

12. Gregory of Tours refers to Hygelac as an historical figure some two centuries before he appears in *Beowulf. The Oxford Companion to English Literature*, 5th edition, (Oxford: OUP, 1985) p. 90.

13. Helen Fielding, *Bridget Jones's Diary* (London and New York: Viking, 1996) is based directly on Jane Austen's *Pride and Prejudice* (1810). It spawned a successful movie and a sequel. Most recently Seth Grahame-Smith has produced *Pride and Prejudice and the Zombies* (Philadelphia: Quirk, 2009), which claims to use about 85 percent of the original text but introduces zombies as a plot element. It is selling briskly. Inspired by this, Ben H. Withers has created *Sense and Sensibility and the Sea Monsters*, also published by Quirk (2009). Not to be out-done Vera Nazarian has produced *Mansfield Park and Mummies: Monster Mayhem, Matrimony, Ancient Curses, True Love, and other Dire Delights* (Winnetka: Curiosities Press, 2009). It, too, has had an enthusiastic response. All three are examples of how a new tale can trade on the reputation of an existing story, and how authors can incorporate trendy elements to ensure success. They are extreme examples, perhaps, and are more interesting as sociology than as observations upon human behavior.

14. Allan Hunter, *Stories We Need to Know* (Scotland: Findhorn, 2008) and *The Six Archetypes of Love* (Scotland: Findhorn, 2008). Both of these books discuss the ubiquity of the six archetypes we'll be referring to here.

15. Carl G. Jung, *Man and His Symbols* (London: Pan, rpt. 1978). Others who have extended Jung's concept of archetypes include Carol Pearson and Sharon Seivert. My own books *Stories We Need to Know* and *The Six Archetypes of Love*, cited above, redress the balance.

16. Information about the pilgrims of New Mexico was supplied by Nicky Leach.

17. Joseph Campbell frequently referred to the work of Adolf Bastian (1826–1905), specifically the concept of *Elementargedanken,* or elementary ideas, which were the basis from which local variations in the expressions of archetypes would spring.

18. Shakespeare's sources for *Romeo and Juliet* also include Luigi Da Porto's story of *Romeo and Giulietta* where its full title is *Historia novellamente ritrovato di due nobili amanti,* (Venice, 1530). This version was translated into English by

Arthur Brooke in 1562, and is considered by Gibbon as "originating in folk-lore". *The Arden Shakespeare: Romeo and Juliet,* ed. Brian Gibbon (Methuen, 1980), pp. 32-33.

19. Joseph Campbell, "the picture language of the soul" appears in *Grimm's Fairy Tales.* op. cit., p. 864.
20. W. H. Auden, quoted on the cover *Grimm's Fairy Tales,* op. cit.
21. Richard Adams, ibid.

## Chapter 1

1. Çatal Hüyük is the site excavated by archaeologist Marija Gimbutas and described in her books, of which *The Civilization of the Goddess* (Harper San Francisco, 1991) is the most extensive. Gimbutas refers to the frog as a regenerative symbol (p. 255) and adds, "As a frog, she is Holla who brings the red apple, the symbol of life, back to earth from the well into which it fell at harvest. Her realm is the inner depth of mounds and caves. This powerful goddess was not erased from the mythical world but lives on throughout Europe as the Baltic Ragana, the Polish Jedza, Mora and Morava from Serbia, the Basque Mari, the Irish Morrigan, and the Russian Baba Yaga." (p. 243). This tantalizing glimpse of a goddess who retrieves objects from wells to ensure fertility, and who is still revered as a "Mother of the Dead" to this day, plays into the themes of "The Frog-King," as we have seen. "The Goddess in the form of a frog or toad predominates in the temples, and her icons or amulets of marble, alabaster, green stone, ivory, or clay are found throughout the Neolithic, Bronze Age, and even throughout historical times" (p. 244). Significantly, Grimm's tale No. 24 is called "Mother Holle" and concerns a young woman who drops her weaving shuttle down a well, is forced to retrieve it from the depths, and is transformed when gold showers down on her as she returns. The echoes are too strong to ignore.

## Chapter 2

1. The shirt of Nessus. Deianeira unwittingly gives the shirt, tainted with the blood of the centaur Nessus, to her husband Hercules, who puts it on and is scorched by it but cannot take it off. In despair, he throws himself on a funeral pyre and dies.
2. Abraham and Isaac. The story is in The Bible, Genesis 22: 1–24.
3. Mark Twain, widely reported quotation. From *www.quotedb.com/quotes/1343.*

## Chapter 4

1. Sting, "Rock Steady" on *The Dream of Blue Turtles*, A&M recordings, 1985.
2. Elisabeth Young-Bruehl's fascinating theories are discussed most persuasively in her collection of essays, *Where Do We Fall When We Fall in Love?* (New York: Other Press, 2003). Young-Bruehl's distinguished status as a researcher and biographer makes her findings persuasive. An interesting sidelight on this topic comes from a sociological survey by Dr. Malcolm Brynin of the University of Essex (UK), which reported that the experience of a passionate first love affair can actually damage individuals in such a way that they believe they will not feel the same degree of attachment and excitement ever again. It was reported on 19 January, 2009. See: *www.redorbit.com/news/oddities/1625350/study_first_love_ can_hurt_future_romance/*
3. Max Luthi, *Once Upon a Time* (Bloomington: Indiana University Press, Midland edition, 1976), pp.118–119.

## Chapter 5

1. "Cinderella's Syndrome" was the name given to the phenomenon of adopted children making false accusations of mistreatment. It was first identified by Dr. Peter K. Lewin in 1976. Subsequently, the "Cinderella Complex" was described by Colette Dowling to identify the tendency of young women to want to be taken care of by others and give up their independence. Her book, *The Cinderella Complex: Women's Hidden Fear of Independence.* (New York: Summit Books, 1981 1990), has popularized the term. As we'll see, neither researcher has a firm grip on the actual tale.
2. The Emo cult is now larger than ever. Violent scenes have erupted in Mexico City at several gatherings of Emo groups who were asking for acceptance and freedom from persecution. Reported on BBC America, News, Nov. 3, 2009.

## Chapter 7

1. A British news article by Ed Pilkington dated Nov. 28, 2009 describes what he calls "Young Guns"- children as young as 5 who are entered in Texas handgun competitions. He mentions 8 year old Sebastian Mann who had recently shot his first deer. *www.guardian.co.uk/society/2009/nov/28/gun-lobby-children-us.* Pilkington mentions InSights magazine as a source for some of this information.

2. At least two articles cover this. This reference is to: "Chastity Bono Undergoing Sex Change," *People Magazine*, July 21, 2009, by Stephen M. Silverman. This news report has now been confirmed by later reports.

## Chapter 8

1. *Extreme Makeover* first aired on ABC in 2002. The *Home Edition* began in 2003 and ran until 2007. *What Not to Wear* currently (2009) has a UK and a US edition (broadcast by TLC), and is also broadcast in Columbia, Argentina, and Canada. *The Biggest Loser* (NBC) first aired in 2004. The eighth season will be in Sept. 2009. It has US, UK, and Australian versions. We could also consider such shows as *How to Look Good Naked,* which first aired in the UK in 2006 on Channel 4. It now has a UK and a US edition, as well as many other variants worldwide. Four UK series appeared up until 2008, and two US series (Lifetime TV).
2. *How Clean is Your House?* BBC America, 2009.
3. *The Elegance of the Hedgehog*, Muriel Barbery, translated by Alison Anderson (New York: Europa Editions, 2008).
4. Marija Gimbutas points out that the hedgehog is a very ancient religious symbol. "Large jars (pithoi) shaped like hedgehogs were also found enclosing the skeletons of infants. Here we have a synthesis of three related symbols: the grave, the womb, and the hedgehog" (op. cit. p. 244). This fits fairly closely with the idea that one aspect of Hans has to "die," so that he can become a full husband to the princess and that within the formidable outer shell is a tender, innocent individual.

## Chapter 12

1. *Beowulf*: the best modern translation is by Seamus Heaney, which is reprinted in *The Norton Anthology of English Literature*, ed. Greenblatt et al., (New York: Norton, 2006), Eighth edition, vol. 1.

## Chapter 13

1. The legend of Orpheus and Eurydice exists in many forms. The version referred to here dates to the time of Virgil (70 B.C.–19 B.C.).
2. The best known legend about the stag is probably that of St. Hubertus who went hunting on Good Friday and met a stag with a crucifix between its horns.

He converted to Christianity on the spot (*Bibliotheca hagiographica Latina* nos. 3994–4002). This idea of the stag as carrying a holy value also appears in the legend of St. Eustace. This may be a very ancient symbol as the scepter found among the Viking/Anglo-Saxon Sutton Hoo treasure in England had a stag figure on top (625 A.D.), and Pazyryk burials of the 5th century B.C. also featured stag bones, while the hall Beowulf protects is called Heorot, the "hall of the hart."

3. Lynn Barber's article appeared in the British Sunday newspaper *The Observer*, June 7, 2009. Reprinted by the Guardian.co.uk as "My Harsh Lesson in Love and Life" *www.guardian.co.uk/culture/2009/jun/07/lynn-barber-virginity-relationships*. The memoir from which the article is extracted, *An Education* (London: Penguin, 2009), has proved popular. This leads one to think the coercive situation she describes has resonance for many women. Barber's memoir has been made into an award winning movie, with a script by Nick Hornby.

## Chapter 14

1. Frank J. Sulloway, *Born To Rebel: Birth Order, Family Dynamics and Creative Lives* (New York: Vintage, 1997).

## Afterword

1. Joseph Campbell is quoted in Sharon Seivert, *The Balancing Act* (Rochester Vt.: Park Street Press, 2001), p. 40.

## Appendix

1. Grimms' use of dialect. Quoted by Padraic Colum in *Grimm*, op. cit. p. viii.
2. Schopenhauer quotation, in Robert Van De Castle, *Our Dreaming Mind* (New York: Ballantine, 1994) pp. 91-92. Van De Castle cites his source as H. Ellenberger, *The Discovery of the Unconscious* (Basic Books, 1970), p. 209.

# SELECT BIBLIOGRAPHY

*Beowulf*, trans. Seamus Heaney. New York: Norton, 2001
**Bettelheim, Bruno.** *The Uses of Enchantment.* New York: Vintage Books, 1977
**Bettelheim, Bruno.** *Symbolic Wounds.* Glencoe, NY: The Free Press, 1954
**Bly, Robert.** *Iron John.* Boston: Addison-Wesley, 1990
**Bottigheimer, R.** *Fairy Tales: A New History.* New York: State University of New York Press, 2009

**Campbell, Joseph.** *The Hero with a Thousand Faces.* London: HarperCollins, 1993
**Campbell, Joseph.** *The Masks of God.* London: Secker and Warburg, 1960
**Castle, Robert Van de.** *Our Dreaming Mind.* New York: Random House, 1994
**Cooper, Jean C.** *Fairy Tales; Allegories of the Inner Life.* Wellingborough, UK: The Aquarian Press, 1983

**Johnson, Robert A.** *The Fisher King and the Handless Maiden.* San Francisco: Harper, 1995
**Johnson, Robert A.** *Owning Your Own Shadow.* San Francisco: Harper, 1996
**Jung, Carl G.** *Man and His Symbols.* London: Pan Books, 1978

**Gadd, Ann.** *Climbing the Beanstalk.* Scotland: Findhorn Press, 2007
**Gimbutas, Marija.** *The Civilization of the Goddess.* Harper San Francisco, 1991
**Grimm, Jacob and Willhelm.** *The Complete Grimm's Fairy Tales.* New York, Pantheon, 1944. Reprinted 1972, introduced by Padraic Colum, and commentary by Joseph Campbell.

**Hunter, Allan G.** *Stories We Need to Know.* Scotland: Findhorn Press, 2008
**Hunter, Allan G.** *The Six Archetypes of Love.* Scotland: Findhorn Press, 2008

**Luthi, Max.** *Once Upon a Time: On the Nature of Fairy Tales.* Bloomington: Indiana University Press, Midland imprint, 1976

**Myss, Caroline.** *Sacred Contracts.* New York: Harmony Books, 2001

**Ovid,** *Metamorphoses.* Trans. Rolfe Humphries. Bloomington: Indiana University Press, 1955

**Perrault, Charles.** *The Complete Fairy Tales of Charles Perrault.* Trans. and ed. Sally Holmes, Nicoletta Simborowski, Neil Philip. New York: Clarion Press, 1993

**Sale, Roger.** *Fairy Tales and After.* Cambridge, MA: Harvard Univ. Press, 1978
**Sulloway, Frank.** *Born To Rebel.* New York: Vintage, 1997

**Whitley, David.** *The Idea of Nature in Disney Animation.* Aldershot: Ashgate, 2008

# Further Allan G. Hunter titles

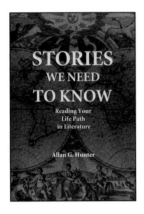 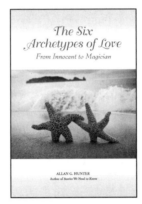 

### STORIES WE NEED TO KNOW

*If you're looking for reliable, time-tested guidance on your journey through life then this is the book for you. Using the wisdom of over three thousand years of literature and myth, Dr. Allan Hunter explores the stories we need to know and understand, and shows how they have offered us real advice and guidance for generations.*

**978-1-84409-123-2**

### THE SIX ARCHETYPES OF LOVE

*Dr. Allan G. Hunter identifies six classic profiles of individuals in love; the Innocent, the Orphan, the Pilgrim, the Warrior-Lover, the Monarch and the Magician. He shows how we can move through and become any one of these archetypes at different stages in our lives and our spiritual development.*

**978-1-84409-142-3**

### WRITE YOUR MEMOIR

*Extending beyond the idea that memoir writing is intended to put past events into a more understandable current perspective, this guide maintains that keeping a document of one's life is actually the basis of a psychic process called "soul work," which manifests as a desire to experience the state of being alive to the fullest.*

**978-1-84409-177-5**

F I N D H O R N   P R E S S

*Life Changing Books*

For a complete catalogue,
please contact:

Findhorn Press Ltd
117-121 High Street,
Forres IV36 1AB,
Scotland, UK

*t* +44 (0)1309 690582
*f* +44 (0)131 777 2711
*e* info@findhornpress.com

or consult our catalogue online
(with secure order facility) on
www.findhornpress.com

For information on the Findhorn Foundation:
www.findhorn.org